Yogic Practices of the Himalayan Tradition

as taught by
H.H. Swami Rama
of the Himalayas

Prakash Keshaviah, Ph.D.

Himalayan Institute Hospital Trust
Swami Ram Nagar, P.O. Jolly Grant
Dehradun 248016 Uttarakhand, India

Cover photograph: Dr. Dushyant Gaur

© 2019 Himalayan Institute Hospital Trust. All rights reserved.

Library of Congress Control Number 2019937436

ISBN 978-81-88157-97-6

Published by:
Himalayan Institute Hospital Trust
Swami Ram Nagar, P.O. Jolly Grant
Dehradun 248016
Uttarakhand, India
tel: 91-135-241-2068, fax: 91-135-247-1612
src@hihtindia.org, www.hihtindia.org

Distributed by Lotus Press, P.O. Box 325, Twin Lakes, WI
53181 U.S.A., www.lotuspress.com, 800-824-6396, lotuspress@
lotuspress.com.

Contents

Acknowledgments

The preparation of this manual has been a team effort and we would like to recognize the members of this team for their valuable contributions:

Cover photo: Dr. Dushyant Gaur
Proofreading: Kamal and Dr. Prakash Keshaviah
Photography: Ajay Lal, Mela Ram and Sons
Yoga model: Rahul Baluni
Book design, layout and production: Kamal
Editing and presentation by: Dr. Prakash Keshaviah

Foreword

The purpose in compiling this book is to create for spiritual aspirants a ready reference of the many *kriyas* (yogic practices, derived from the Sanskrit *kri,* to act) of the Himalayan tradition that H.H. Swami Rama taught his students during the more than two decades that he spent in the United States. The vast majority of kriyas were taught by Swamiji during seminars, workshops and lectures and have found their way into the books authored by Swamiji. However, they are scattered through many books and there is no ready reference where all of these kriyas are compiled and presented. It is hoped that this volume will serve that purpose. Fortunately, many of the kriyas were personally taught to the compiler of this volume during small group sessions, seminars and workshops and the writings have been compiled from his notes. The reader of this manual will derive greater benefit from first studying the beginning level *Holistic Living Manual* and practicing the guided practices in the 2-volume audio series, "Basic Practices of the Himalayan Tradition."

As Swamiji always reminded us, the purpose of human life is to attain a state that confers true happiness, bereft of all pains, miseries and bondages. The prescription for purposeful living may be simply summarized below:

- Nourish and exercise the body
- Make the breath deep and even
- Discipline the senses

- Quieten the mind
- Calm the emotions
- Realize the Divinity within you.

Note: Italicized words are defined in the Glossary.

Chapter 1
Introduction

"The time has come for man to realize that he is not body alone. He is a breathing being and a thinking being too — a unique individual made up of complex emotions, appetites and desires."

Swami Rama, *A Practical Guide to Holistic Health*

Swami Rama created a simple but profound model of a human being as shown in Figure 1. Integration of an individual requires integration of body, breath, mind, and Atman (soul or center of consciousness). The body becomes aware of the world outside because of the *jnanendriyas,* the five organs of sensory perception. In reaction to the sensory stimuli received from the outside world, the body reacts through the *karmendriyas,* the five active organs of speech, locomotion, grasping, reproduction and elimination. This constant interplay between the body and the outside world keeps the mind outer-directed and unaware of the center of consciousness from which it derives its power and intelligence.

The ancient sages of India had identified four main aims in human life *(purusharthas),* namely, *dharma* (ethical codes that form the foundation of society), *kama* (literally desire, referring to fulfillment of sensual urges), *artha* (material prosperity) and *moksha* (spiritual emancipation). In keeping with these major aims of life, they formulated four *ashramas* or life stages, *brahmacharya, grihasta, vanaprastha* and *sannyasa*. The first stage of the student (brahmacharya) was for studying the codes of dharma and for acquisition of knowledge and life skills. This first stage required self-discipline and avoiding the distractions of sensory pleasures. It was, therefore, usually done in a forest ashram under the mentorship of a guru. Having completed the first stage, the student now returned to the main stream, entering the second stage of the householder (grihasta), taking a spouse and raising a family. The second stage of the householder was for satisfaction of the sensual urges (kama) and for acquisition of material prosperity (artha) using the life skills learnt as a student and being guided by the codes of dharma. Once the householder had fulfilled family responsibilities and had sated material and sensory needs, the third stage of the forest dweller (vanaprastha) commenced. This stage signifies getting disentangled from family and worldly ties, leaving the mainstream and retiring to a study of the scriptures and the acquisition of wisdom, untrammeled by the pull of the senses and the longing for material comforts. When the aspirant was ripe, the fourth stage of renunciation (sannyasa) was undertaken with total dedication to the spiritual life and the pursuit of realization (moksha).

Just as the four stages of life prepared one to systematically advance from student to sannyasi in search of moksha, so too, by analogy, does the eight-limbed *(ashtanga)* science of *Raja Yoga* take the *sadhaka* (spiritual aspirant) in a systematic progression from the first step of sadhana to the summit of samadhi. Raja Yoga has a scientific, logical, systematic and sequential approach for making the mind inward-directed, in order to discover the source of peace and bliss.

The five *yamas* or restraints (non-hurting, non-lying, non-indulgence in sensuality, non-stealing, and non-attachment) are designated as the first limb. The five *niyamas* or observances (purity, contentment, practices for self-discipline, study of the scriptures and surrender

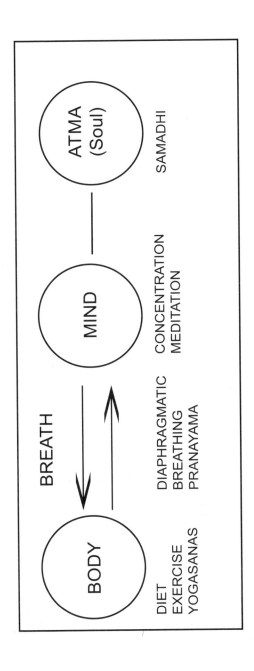

Figure 1

to the higher power) connote the second limb. The yamas and niyamas are analogous to the codes of dharma that the student had to master in the first stage. The practice of *tapas* (practices for self-discipline) and *swadhyaya* (study of the scriptures) are also analogous to the studies undertaken in the first stage of life. Many descriptions of the eight-limbed Raja Yoga use the analogy of a ladder, the eight limbs being the eight rungs (Figure 2A). As the yamas and niyamas form the lowest two rungs of the ladder, the sadhaka might be disheartened if he is required to master the yamas and niyamas before proceeding further on the path of Raja Yoga.

An alternate representation might be more appropriate. A ladder has horizontal rungs and two vertical columns that not only provide hand-hold support but also serve to keep the rungs in place. With this representation (Figure 2B), one realizes that the yamas and niyamas provide support and stability throughout the spiritual journey until one reaches the summit. The yamas and niyamas provide support, self-discipline and purification for successfully ascending to the summit. The yamas and niyamas constitute the dharmic code for the spiritual aspirant.

The yamas and the niyamas along with the third limb of *asana* (posture) and the fourth limb of *pranayama* (regulation and expansion of the vital energy), constitute the four limbs of *Hatha Yoga,* the outer yoga. The limbs of asana and pranayama deal with the body and vital energy and are, by analogy, like the householder stage of sadhana. The householder is learning to deal with the outer world. Similarly, asana and pranayama are necessary to discipline the outer sheaths of food (physical body) and *prana* (vital energy). The acquisition of material prosperity is analogous to the acquisition of good bodily health and making the body a fit instrument for the ultimate goal. The satisfaction of sensory urges is, by analogy similar to the limb of pranayama as it is the same vitality of prana that

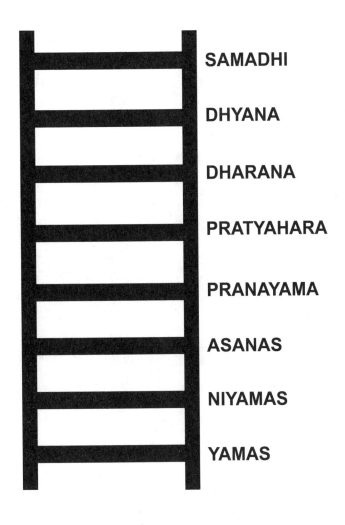

Figure 2A

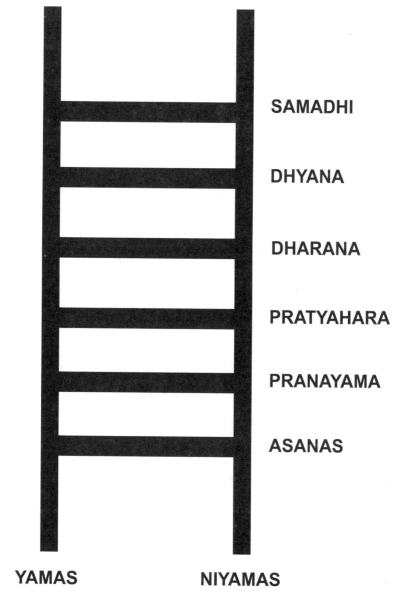

Figure 2B

can manifest as sensual urges, or can, by regulation, lead beyond the senses. The asanas and pranayama not only serve to keep the body healthy, making it a fit instrument for achieving the purpose of life, but also facilitate stillness. The Bible declares, "Be still and know that you are God." Stillness of the mind has to be preceded by stillness of the body and serenity of the breath. Asanas and pranayama promote this stillness.

The last four rungs, the inner yoga, are *pratyahara* (sensory withdrawal), *dharana* (concentration), *dhyana* (meditation) and *samadhi* (Self-realization). Pratyahara and dharana may be taken to be analogous to the third stage of the forest dweller. Just as the forest dweller is trying to disentangle himself from worldly affairs and material comforts, the sadhaka is trying to disentangle himself from sensory distractions by practicing pratyahara. Just as the householder is disciplining the body and senses by withdrawing from the mainstream, dharana or concentration is to discipline the wandering mind and withdraw it from worldly affairs of the outer life to the inner seeking. The last two rungs of dhyana (meditation) and samadhi are by analogy comparable to the last life stage of sannyasa where the inner life takes over completely. In dhyana, there is no longer an object to fix one's mind upon. The thinking process is being curtailed. In sannyasa, there are no worldly ties or encumbrances to engage one. All other activities have been curtailed. Ultimately, samadhi or moksha is the crowning glory of life for both the sannyasi and for the sadhaka.

The chapters of this handbook are arranged in the step-wise progression of the limbs of Raja Yoga, this being the logical progression for the various stages of the sadhaka in his inner quest. Chapter 2 deals with asanas and kriyas for making the body capable of stillness to facilitate spiritual progress. The emphasis here is not merely on bodily health but on facilitating spiritual growth.

It is interesting to note the interplay of body and mind. As Swamiji would often tell us, "All of the body is in the mind, but not all of the mind is in the body." It has been observed that one who is rigid and not open to other points of view also suffers from rigidity of the limbs and joints. Conversely, limbering the body, making the limbs supple and the joints free of stiffness and pain, automatically opens up the mind making it more flexible and able to appreciate other points of view. Also, changing one's body image helps one change one's mode of thinking and approach to issues and challenges. Swami Rama emphasized that habits are formed in childhood. Parents need to teach children the basics of good posture, diaphragmatic breathing, nutritious food, proper chewing of food and toilet habits. The body builds toxins from bad food, bad posture, bad habits and bad thinking.

Chapter 3 explains the role of prana, the vital energy, in spiritual sadhana. The breath is more vital than food. Breath is a vehicle, the horse, whose rider is prana, the vital energy. Prana enters the body through the breath. Breath is life. All the body cells are floating in air. There is air within and without. Breath awareness and other breathing techniques help overcome lassitude and create energy. During sleep, if breathing is bad, one does not get good rest. The pause between inhalation and exhalation is death. As Swami Rama has explained, an extended pause between inhalation and exhalation causes coronary artery disease. The yogi who controls the pause controls death.

The respiratory system directly or indirectly influences all other body systems. To be successful, one needs to build a strong bridge between external life and internal life. Breathing techniques can help build this bridge. Ramana Maharshi, the great sage of South India, in his work, *Upadesha Saram (Essence of Instruction)*, has declared unequivocally that breath and mind branch off from a common source, shakti or primal energy. He asserts that just as a bird is restrained by a net, so too can the mind be stilled by regulation of the breath. Once the mind's wandering has been constrained by regulation of the breath, the thinking process can be completely annihilated by single-minded attention to the Self. As Swami Rama used to say, "Mind and breath are inseparable like the letters 'q' and 'u.' " In the model provided by Swami Rama, the breath is the link between body and mind. When this link is broken, we call it death. Swamiji was fond of telling us that the breath is the barometer of the mind. One's emotions are reflected in the breath. Anger makes the breath uneven and jerky. A sudden shock is accompanied by a sharp intake of breath. Sighing out of grief or depression is associated with a prolonged exhalation and shallow breathing. There is reciprocity between breath and mind. As breath and mind are two sides of the same coin, one can work on emotions by working on one's breathing. Making the breath serene induces serenity of mind. One becomes responsible, that is able to choose one's responses. One is pro-active rather than reactive. It is therefore appropriate that when one is angry, taking a deep breath and counting to 10 helps one condition one's response to the provocation rather than blindly reacting and repenting later, as the proverb declares, "Act in haste, repent at leisure."

The techniques of pranayama described in Chapter 4 of this handbook help to still the mind and also produce many beneficial results:

- Diaphragmatic breathing is helpful during an emotional crisis. The crocodile posture is a good posture to learn diaphragmatic breathing. One should practice diaphragmatic breathing, twice a day for 15 minutes per session.

- Alternate nostril breathing also helps in controlling emotions and is preliminary to *sushumna application*. Before meditation, both nostrils should be activated by alternate nostril breathing, followed by sushumna application.
- Sushumna application is essential for a tranquil and joyful meditation. Without sushumna application, meditation is a joke! With sushumna application, the breath becomes very fine and subtle. As a consequence, all involuntary muscles like the muscles of the heart and internal muscles get rested.
- *Bhastrika* or bellows helps shake the jars of the lungs, clearing the inaccessible corners of the lungs.

The four bad habits of breathing that need to be avoided are:

- Shallow breathing, with inhalation and exhalation being unequal
- Jerky breathing
- Noisy breathing, caused by blockage of the nasal passages
- Pause between inhalation, exhalation and the next inhalation.

In Chapter 5, several kriyas are presented which are labeled as relaxation exercises. However, they are more profound than simple relaxation. The benefits derived from these kriyas go beyond relaxing the gross muscles and joints. They relax even the smooth muscles of the circulatory system and provide deep rest to the body, resulting in lowered heart and respiration rates, lowered blood pressure, lowered blood sugar and a lowering of the basal metabolic rate.

In the spiritual context, with the kriyas of Chapter 5, one is working with the fifth limb of Raja Yoga, namely pratyahara or withdrawal of the senses. The senses may be viewed as the tentacles of consciousness that are outward directed. Pratyahara reverses the direction, allowing the mind to become inward-directed. In the Hindu scripture called the Bhagavad Gita, pratyahara is described through the analogy of a tortoise drawing its limbs into its protective shell when faced with danger. The outward wandering senses, the tentacles of consciousness reaching out into the world, pose dangers to the spiritual aspirant, the dangers of getting enmeshed in sensual indulgences and worldly affairs. There are no treatises or elaborate commentaries on pratyahara. Pratyahara can be experienced through the techniques described in Chapter 5. These techniques provide protection by disciplining the senses and directing them inward. If the senses are not disciplined and directed inwards, one will not be able to proceed to the next limb of Raja Yoga, namely dharana or concentration.

Chapter 6, titled, "Going Beyond," presents kriyas that encompass the last three limbs of Raja Yoga, namely dharana (concentration), dhyana (meditation) and samadhi (realization). Dharana is making the mind one-pointed. For focusing the mind, one needs an object of concentration. In the kriyas of Chapter 6, the mind is focused on the breath, or on an energy center, or on specific visualizations.

When concentration is sustained and prolonged, it develops into meditation. The traditional analogy used is that of the steady, unbroken flow of a stream of oil. When water flows, it may break up into droplets with gaps in between. Oil is viscous and the viscous nature of oil prevents its breakup, so that the stream is unbroken and steady.

When the mind drifts away from the object of concentration, gaps occur between thoughts. In meditation, the gaps are closed. Putting it differently, the gap between thoughts is penetrated and expanded so that there are no thoughts and no gaps. Meditation is described in Sanskrit as *nirvishayam*, that is without an object. Concentration requires an object but in meditation, one goes beyond objects and beyond thoughts.

The kriyas like the 61 point exercise and *shitali karana* are preliminaries to the practice of *yoga nidra*. Yoga nidra, or yogic sleep has also been described as sleepless sleep or conscious sleep. As Swamiji tells us, two people go to see a king. One falls asleep and is oblivious to the grandeur of the palace and the magnificence of the king. He is in the presence of the king but not aware of his majesty. That is like the state of deep sleep. One is close to the center of consciousness but separated by the thin veil of the causal sheath. In yoga nidra, one is visiting the same palace and sitting before the same king, but one is fully conscious, fully aware of the grandeur of the palace and the majesty of the king. The very simple but subtle *OM kriya* takes one to the fringes of samadhi and complements the practice of yoga nidra.

The Mandukya Upanishad, the tersest but most profound of Upanishads, deals with the four states of consciousness: waking, dreaming, deep sleep and *turiya*, the fourth state, beyond the three commonly experienced states. In Swami Rama's commentary on the Mandukya *(OM, the Eternal Witness)*, he describes seven states of consciousness (Figure 3). He identifies the transitional states between waking and dreaming *(unmani)*, between dreaming and deep sleep *(ahladini)* and between deep sleep and turiya (samadhi). This transitional state of samadhi is not a trance-like state nor is it a blank state like that induced by anesthesia. In the lower samadhi there is still some sense of duality. In

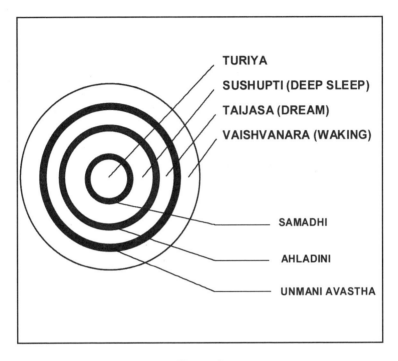

TURIYA

SUSHUPTI (DEEP SLEEP)

TAIJASA (DREAM)

VAISHVANARA (WAKING)

SAMADHI

AHLADINI

UNMANI AVASTHA

Figure 3

the higher samadhi, there is the experience of only One, without a second. It is a fully conscious, all-knowing state. This is the state of turiya. Swamiji has assured us that the sincere and dedicated practice of these kriyas will take us beyond, hence the title of Chapter 6, "Going Beyond."

As St. Francis has so beautifully stated, it is in giving that we receive. By giving and sharing the teachings of Swami Rama of the Himalayas, may we all receive the grace of the Himalayan sages.

OM shanti, shanti, shantihi.

Chapter 2
Stilling the Body

Asana or posture is the third limb of Raja Yoga. There are two types of asanas—meditative asanas and asanas for physical well-being. In Patanjali's Yoga Sutras, there is no detailed exposition of asana other than to state that asana should be *sthira* (steady) and *sukha* (comfortable). Just learning to be still in a quiet place makes the mind peaceful and joyous. The mind and body interact to an amazing degree. If the posture is unsteady, the mind becomes restless. Conversely, when the body is made still, the mind starts to become calm, resulting in peace and joy.

Figure 4

The corpse pose is deeply relaxing and excellent for practicing breath awareness.

Shavasana, the Corpse Pose

Many of the kriyas in this book will be performed in *shavasana. Shava,* in Sanskrit, means corpse. It is said that if from Shiva, the divine male principle of consciousness, the 'i,' symbolic of the divine female principle is removed, what remains is shava or corpse.

In the corpse posture, one lies on one's back, with the heels spread about shoulder width apart (see Figure 4). The hands are placed comfortably on either side, without touching the sides of the body. The palms are turned upwards and the fingers are relaxed and gently curled upwards. It is advisable to use a thin cushion or folded blanket to support the head and neck. This slight elevation of the upper part of the body will prevent any disturbance from digestive gases. If you experience pain in the lower back in this posture, a rolled-up mat or blanket can be positioned below the knees to provide support. To prevent your getting cold during the practice, a light sheet or blanket can be used to cover the body. The eyes are gently closed during practices in this posture. If the ambient light is distracting, a dark colored (black or red) blindfold can be used. If there are distracting noises, suitable ear plugs may be used. However, one of the reasons for doing many of these kriyas is to develop pratyahara or sensory withdrawal. So light and sounds will pose less disturbance as one develops the ability to withdraw the senses from the surroundings. Relax the entire body and feel the weight of the body being supported by the floor along the length of the body. Bring your awareness to your breath and make sure that you are breathing diaphragmatically, the breath being deep and free of sound, jerks and pauses.

The corpse posture allows one to achieve a very deep state of relaxation. There is decreased tone of the sympathetic nervous system and increased tone of the para-sympathetic system, thus reducing stress and anxiety and producing a calm and relaxed feeling. The whole nervous system is strengthened by the practice of relaxation in the corpse posture and one's mental capacity increases. Muscles become more efficient because of the relaxation induced by this posture. In addition, the venous circulation improves and fatigue is relieved. Both the rate of respiration and the heart rate decrease and there is lowering of the blood pressure and load on the heart. The rate of basal metabolism is also concomitantly decreased. With the body being relaxed and the breath becoming serene, the mind also becomes quieter.

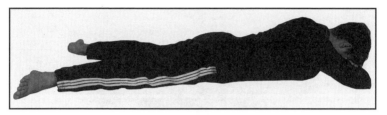

Figure 5

Makarasana, the Crocodile Posture

This posture is very useful in learning how to breathe diaphragmatically. In this posture, one lies on the floor on one's stomach (Figure 5). The arms are folded at the elbow and the hands grasp the opposite biceps. The folded arms are placed on the floor with the forehead resting on the folded arms. The positioning of the folded arms on the floor is adjusted such that the upper body, above the navel, is off the floor. The abdomen rests comfortably against the floor. The heels are spread apart and may be turned inwards or outwards according to one's preference and feeling of comfort.

Become aware of your breathing while in this posture. To avoid breathing dust off the floor, a clean piece of cloth can be positioned beneath the nostrils. In the crocodile posture, as one breathes, one becomes aware of the movement of the abdominal wall. During exhalation the pressure of the abdomen against the floor reduces and during inhalation, one feels increased pressure between the abdomen and the floor. The floor thus provides a feedback mechanism regarding the correct technique of diaphragmatic breathing. Also, the position of the arms with the forehead resting on the folded arms inhibits the tendency for chest breathing.

Diaphragmatic breathing is easily learnt in the crocodile posture. A deep sense of relaxation is induced while breathing diaphragmatically in this posture. Make sure that your breathing is deep, quiet, smooth and free of pauses between exhalation and inhalation.

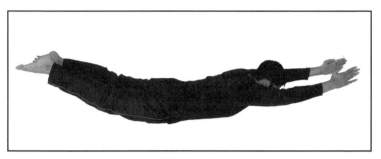

Figure 6

The Boat Posture

Lie down on the floor on your stomach. Keeping the feet about a foot and a half apart, and the arms parallel to each other and alongside the ears, raise the arms and legs off the floor with an inhalation (Figure 6). Feel the weight of the body with only the navel touching the floor. In this posture, the body configuration assumes the smooth curve of a boat, with the arms slightly lower than the legs. Hold the pose for about five seconds, breathing normally. Lower the body with an exhalation. Repeat the posture two more times.

In this posture, the muscles of the back are strengthened and the circulation to the abdominal viscera is increased.

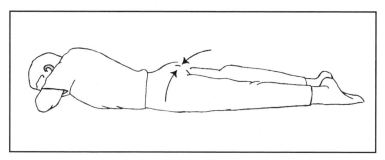

Figure 7

Ashwini Mudra

To start with, assume the crocodile posture but with the feet together. Slowly and without jerks, roll the buttocks inwards as if the anus is retracting into the rectum. Tighten the muscles trying to flatten and firm up the buttocks (Figure 7). With practice, an inward movement of more than six to nine inches can be achieved. Hold for a few seconds and then release the tension, relaxing the buttocks. Repeat the mudra a second time. In a few weeks, once the mudra has become easy, it can be practiced in the standing position. This mudra is good for toning the muscles of the buttocks. It is also a preliminary to the *muladhara bandha* or root lock that is held during meditation.

The Child's Pose

Sit in a kneeling position on the floor with the buttocks resting on the heels. Keeping the head, neck and trunk straight, relax the arms and rest the hands on the floor, palms upward and fingers pointing to the back (Figure 8A).

Now with a slow exhalation, bend forward at the hips till the forehead touches the floor with the stomach and chest resting on the thighs. As you bend forward, let the hands slide back into a comfortable position. Keep the buttocks resting on the heels (Figure 8B).

In this position, you will notice that as you inhale, the abdomen will press against the thighs. This pressure will be released during exhalation.

This posture is used to place the intestines into the right position in the abdomen. To do this, take five vigorous breaths, with the abdomen being forcefully drawn in during exhalation and being pressed against the thighs during inhalation. After the vigorous breaths, slowly resume the kneeling position with the buttocks resting on the heels.

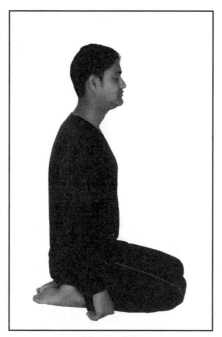

Figure 8A

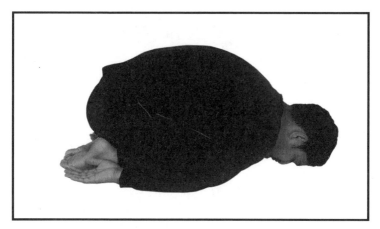

Figure 8B

Seated Postures for the
Practice of Pranayama and Meditation

Figure 9

Maitreyi Asana (Friendship Pose)

This is the posture for those who are unable to sit cross-legged on the floor. Sit on a straight-backed wooden chair, with the head, neck and trunk aligned and erect. Rest your palms on the knees. Keep your feet firmly planted on the floor (Figure 9). If your feet do not reach the floor, use a cushion on the floor to rest your feet.

Figure 11

Figure 10

Sukhasana (Easy Pose)

Sit on the edge of a folded blanket in order to align the head, neck and trunk and keep the back erect. Keeping the head, neck and trunk aligned and erect is important for the flow of prana. This posture is the easiest cross-legged posture. Place the left foot underneath the right knee and the right foot beneath the left knee. Each knee is supported by the opposite foot. Rest the hands on the knees (Figure 10). The finger lock may be used (Figure 11). This posture is comfortable for those who are not used to sitting cross-legged on the floor. It is also advised for those with knee joint problems. However, the posture does not have the stability of the other meditative postures that employ the foot lock.

Figure 12

Swastikasana (Auspicious Pose)

Sit on the edge of a folded blanket in order to align the head, neck and trunk and keep the back erect. Bend the left knee and place the sole of the left foot along the right thigh. Bend the right knee and place the right foot on the left calf. Lock the right foot in between the left thigh and left calf, with only the right big toe being visible. Pull the toe of the left foot between the right thigh and right calf, making the toe visible. Place the hands on the knees with the finger lock (Figure 12).

Figure 13

Siddhasana (Accomplished Pose)

This is the seated posture favored by adepts in yoga. Once it becomes comfortable through practice, it is very stable and one can sit in it for long periods of time. Sit on the edge of a folded blanket in order to align the head, neck and trunk and keep the back erect. In this posture, the left leg is bent at the knee and the left heel is placed at the perineum (between the anus and the genitals) applying the root lock by contracting and pulling in the anal sphincter. The right knee is bent and the heel placed at the pubic bone, above the genitals. Arrange the legs and feet so that the ankles are aligned and touching each other. Insert the toes of the right foot in between the left thigh and calf, with only the big toe visible. Pull the toes of the left foot up between the right thigh and calf, making the big toe visible (Figure 13). Make sure that the head, neck and trunk are aligned and erect. Rest the hand on the knees with the finger lock.

Figure 14

Padmasana (Lotus Posture)

This is the most stable of the cross-legged postures but may not be the most comfortable for beginners. It is not generally recommended as a meditative posture as it is difficult to apply the root lock in this position. Only very advanced yogis use it as a meditative posture. Sit on the edge of a folded blanket in order to align the head, neck and trunk and keep the back erect. Slowly bend the left knee and place the left foot firmly against the right groin with the sole upturned. Similarly, place the right foot against the left groin with the sole upturned (Figure 14). Both the heels should press against the abdomen. Try to keep the knees as close to the floor as is comfortable. Apply the finger lock.

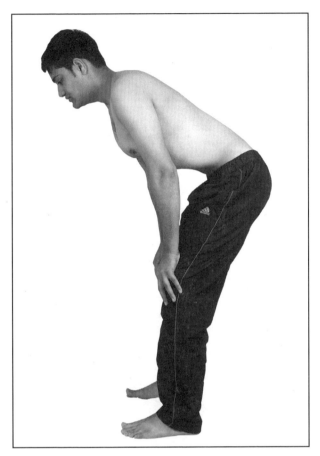

Figure 15A

Agnisara

H.H. Swami Rama would often say that if one did not have time to do any other exercise, one should at least make time to do *agnisara*. It can cure many diseases and energizes the solar system of the body. Agnisara has a beneficial effect on the bowels, bladder, digestive system, nervous system, circulation and reproductive organs.

Agnisara should not be confused with the stomach lift which focuses only on the navel center, nor should it be

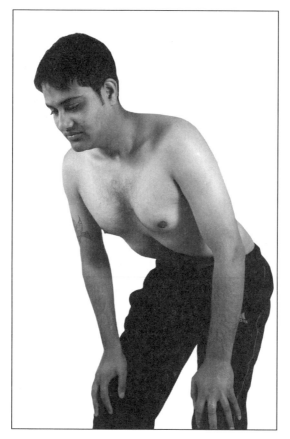

Figure 15B

confused with another practice, a variation of the stomach lift, which is described in Hatha Yoga books as agnisara. Agnisara involves the lower abdomen and entire pelvic region. The pelvis is the lowest portion of the abdomen, from just below the navel to the pubic bone. The pelvic floor is lifted in the proper practice of agnisara.

Stand with your feet comfortably apart, bend at the waist with the back relaxed, resting the weight of the body by placing the hands on the knees (Figure 15A). Apply the root lock and with the exhalation, contract the muscles of the lower abdomen and the area above the pelvis, pulling them in and upwards. Continue the exhalation with the contraction moving upward in a wave-like motion involving the entire abdominal wall (Figure 15B). There is no retention of breath and inhalation follows, with first release of the muscles of the navel and then of the lower abdomen and pelvic region in a downward wave of relaxation.

To begin with, do the kriya about 10-12 times. Gradually increase the number to 50 or more, according to your capacity. Stop and rest if you become short of breath or get tired. Agnisara can be practiced twice a day. This kriya should not be done during menstruation or by pregnant women.

Note: There is a more advanced variation of agnisara which involves application of the *uddiyana bandha* (navel lock) and retention of the breath with the *jalandhara bandha* (chin lock). This advanced variation has to be learnt from a competent teacher and is beyond the scope of this manual.

Chapter 3
Prana, the Vital Link between Body and Mind

(From *OM, the Eternal Witness* by Swami Rama with some minor editing.)

Prana means life and life means prana in the external world. Our everyday experience is that we cannot live without prana. We receive prana through food, we receive prana through our breath, and we even receive prana through our pores. There are many agencies through which we receive prana. Now this prana is always in touch with its source, the original prana, *adi-prana*, the first unit of life. It is through the agency of adi-prana that *Brahman* manifests all the animate and inanimate objects of the world. With the help of that first unit of life, this entire universe comes into existence. Mind, the consciousness manifested in living beings, animate beings, is the agent of the supreme prana. But even inanimate objects are projected, i.e., manifested, by the original prana which is also called *Maya*. We are not talking of the breath, which becomes the vehicle for prana, to supply energy for internal states.

Breath is a projection of the mind. The breath you inhale is called prana, but actually breath is not prana. Breath is called *vayu*, air, in Sanskrit. We find air everywhere, but it is not breath. Because, for breath, there should be something living and conscious to direct it. This vayu is like *ashwa*, a horse. A horse cannot go to its destination unless there is a rider. There is a rider on this breath we are inhaling, called prana; otherwise it's only vayu. Vayu is the horse and prana the rider who directs it. So prana is something living; it's not mere dead air, it's not just a mixture of oxygen, nitrogen and other gases. No, there is a conscious entity called prana that is riding on vayu and leading it.

Now let us try to understand more about this prana that we inhale. You can live without food for many days, but you cannot live without breathing for even a few minutes. A yogi can, through practice, become *aparna*, one who lives only on air. He can live for a long time by taking prana from the air, without taking any solid foods. We get prana through food, but the prana that is supplied by food is not enough; it is not complete. So we receive prana through breath. Breath is a vehicle to supply prana. There are vehicles within, mainly two vehicles, inhalation and exhalation, called prana and *apana*. Now they are doing their duties. However, the mind is definitely superior to these two vehicles. Sometimes mind may get disgusted and condemn and reject you. But prana will never deny you, never reject you, no matter who you are or what you do. Even if you are the worst specimen of humanity, prana will not deny you. Why? Because prana is our mother. No matter what happens, a real mother will never abandon her infant child. She will protect her at any cost, without any discrimination. For her, a child is a child. Mind is like a father. What does a father do? If a son wants some money from his father, the father will ask, "How much do you want?" Five, ten, twenty, one hundred, there is always some limitation. But mother never says I will give you only so much milk, and no more. Take as much as you want, no conditions. So as an infant, you have an unconditional relationship with your mother.

So prana is like our mother. Father is like our mind that discriminates. Mother and father live together, they have a close relationship. Breath and mind are called twin laws of life. To understand mind, you will have to understand your breath. To understand your breath, you will have to understand your mind.

Now, suppose I say OM, and concentrate here, where the upper lip meets the nostrils. The breath will be very fine. Breath will not be shallow, but will be very subtle. Shallow breathing is not good for you, but a yogi's interpretation is that the breath has become very subtle or very fine because he has withdrawn consciously and started breathing subtly. Sant Jnaneshwar, one of the greatest yogis, born in Maharashtra just a few hundred years ago, says, "You are the string of breath and you can easily go from this prana to the other prana, adi prana." The first unit of life, is called prana and the breath is also called prana. That which helps in manifesting this world is prana, that which helps in manifesting *jivas*, souls, is called Brahman. There is a difference. Prana manifested the world but not human souls. I am talking of manifestation, not creation. From One, two, three, four, five, many, can be manifested; this is manifestation of the One becoming many. Suppose you are sitting in a dome of many colors. All the colors have been manifested from only one color, white; this is called manifestation of one. So Brahman is responsible for the manifestation of individual souls, just as the ocean is responsible for the manifestation of waves. So there is a difference between the Brahman who manifests the jivas or the individual souls, and Maya which manifests the universe of objects. Prana and Maya are one and the same. Adi prana is the origin of the prana we are exhaling and inhaling.

What is the relation between this prana we are inhaling and exhaling and that original prana that manifested the universe? There is a relationship. Draw a straight line. You, the individual self, are at one end of the Reality, and the other end is called Absolute Truth. If the two ends of the line are brought together into a circle, then you are one with the Absolute, you can never be separated from the Reality. Have you observed that in many traditions, rings are exchanged as a symbol of marriage, of bride and groom coming together as one? So also, jiva and Brahman are made one, united, and that is called yoga, that unification is called yoga. So what is this marriage? Yoga or union, is the marriage, where the individual soul is made aware of the Reality, made aware that the ultimate goal is to become one with the Reality that is within, not far away.

Pure concentration is when one thought continues for a long time, without intervening thoughts. How can one thought flow continuously? If something is very pleasing to the mind, then the mind likes to flow in that pleasant groove. Mind means energy, and this energy flows through the many grooves of habit patterns. What can you do? You can consciously make new grooves, so that the mind stops flowing through the old grooves and flows through the new channels that you have created. It is a new training program for the mind, a method of transformation.

Now let us study the breath in depth. If you get some bad news, which affects your mind, you may start crying. You may even faint and become unconscious. The bad news may even affect your heart and cause heart failure. How does it happen? What happens to your breath? If you study this whole process, you'll understand how wonderful and unique it is. It will be very useful for you to understand something about your breath. Many people are very particular about their diet and that is good. But no matter how wonderful your diet is, you will not be healthy if you do not learn how to breathe. Pranas play their own important part. When you receive the bad news, the breath is not serene. No, it becomes very shallow. Shallowness of breath is very close to death. Shallow breath is related to an imbalanced mind. Whenever you are imbalanced, whenever you are agitated from within, whenever you are emotional, whenever you are irresponsible, you will find that your breath has become shallow. Not fine, but shallow. Fine breath is made consciously; shallow breath is made by your bad habits. Then you do not fill up to the depth of your lungs and breath becomes very shallow. And during that time, mind does not know what to do, mind becomes weak, because you are not supplying the proper energy; the right volume of blood is not going from the pumping station called the heart to the brain. You will find the same condition, if somebody hits you or gives you a karate chop. There will be a loss of blood supply to the brain. And during that time, the brain does not function well. You may be very powerful and strong, but if hit by a person who has the right training in the martial arts, the right balance, you will become uncoordinated and look in the wrong direction and will not be able to use your physical strength properly.

The mind can make your breath shallow. The mind is a catalogue of habit patterns. Habit patterns are created in the mind because of repeated actions, repeated speech, repeated thoughts, repeated foods, repetitions in our daily life. So when I hear some bad news, that impulse directly affects my mind and my mind immediately, from within, starts crying, and tears start flowing from my eyes. The mind can destroy the body, can make the body unhealthy or miserable. Why? The whole of the body is in the mind, but the whole of the mind is not in the body, this is the underlying principle. To know the whole of the mind, you will have to understand more about the mind. The whole of the body can be understood better through the mind. There is a way of understanding the body through the mind, not mind though body.

If you do not allow your breath to become shallow, whenever such a situation arises, you will not cry, you will not sob, you will not become sad, you will not be grief-stricken. For being sad and sorrowful, your breath has to be shallow. That's why it is said, "Don't have shallow breath." Learn not to have shallow breath, not to have jerky breath, not to create a long pause between inhalation and exhalation. This pause is a key point, because pause is death. Suppose I inhale and never exhale, I am dead; if I inhale and never exhale, I am dead. All the yogic kriyas, all these practices and exercises are done, to control that pause. If you are able to control the pause between inhalation and exhalation, you are a great yogi. An advanced yogi is one who knows how to control the pause between inhalation and exhalation. Pause means death. Death is constantly hovering at the gate of life, but you can keep death away; you can stop her knocking at the door of your life if you do not allow that pause to be increased or expanded unconsciously.

What is the best way to regulate your breath? Sometimes you can measure your breath, but this will happen only when you have knowledge of the *tattwas* or elements. Your body is a compound of five elements, namely, earth, water, fire, air and space. Sometimes the earth element is predominant, sometimes the water element, and so on. The predominant element will definitely affect your breath. Take a piece of mirror and exhale onto it and observe the pattern formed on the surface by the vapor in your exhaled breath. It might, for example, create a moon shape for you, but if you repeat the experiment after an hour or two, you will find that the shape has changed, because a different tattwa is predominant now. In the mountains, the yogis do not have sophisticated machines for experiments, but they know the right experiments! You'll find that the vapor coming out of your mouth makes different shapes because of the influence of tattwas. One day you may find your body is aching all over; this is the influence of vayu tattwa, the air element. On another day, you may feel very hot; this is the influence of the fire tattwa. Now, how to regulate the breath?

Whenever any shocking thing happens, become conscious of your breath and keep it from becoming shallow. How can you make your children strong? You have to be strong, if you want your children to be strong. Strength comes from within, and that strength comes from balance. The more you learn how to have balance in your life, the stronger you will become.

Only a yogi can know which element is predominant by internally observing his breath. But at least you can watch your mind and breath. If your breath is calm, it becomes easy to calm the mind. The most balanced period of your life is when you can establish balance in your mind, in your breath and in your body. For that the five tattwas have to be in balance. You should not allow any one tattwa, one element, to become predominant. How can you do that? It is not easy to manipulate your tattwas, but you can work with the breath. Breath is the barometer of both your mind and body. It's a bridge between the two shores of body and mind; and it's not something dead; it's something living because there is someone directing it. The day that someone withdraws the prana, there will be air but there will not be life; life is not mere breath. Life is prana and prana is life.

When you sit down to meditate, you should first compose yourself, make yourself calm. Just saying, "calm down" is not enough; that calmness does not last for a long time. Is there any other way? Yes. It is called sushumna awakening. What I am going to tell you is based on experiments, based on experience.

Before meditation, you have to learn to make your pranas, the pranic sheath, serene. Look at this point between the nostrils, where the upper lip meets the nostrils. That should be the point of focus to compose yourself and make the breath serene. If you are able to do that, then you will be able to awaken your *sushumna*. In a scientific way, sushumna awakening is very important. Sushumna awakening means that all three channels of energy, *ida, pingala* and sushumna are active. Normally, there are only two active channels, one channel of energy flows though your left nostril (ida), another channel of energy flows through your right nostril (pingala). Experiments have been conducted in many universities showing that flow through the right nostril will give warmer air and that through the left nostril, cooler air, because the electrical potentials of the two nostrils are different, their nature is entirely different. Suppose this nostril of mine is closed. I can open it up by concentrating on it. It will start flowing. Any nostril that is blocked can be made active by concentration on it. It means concentration on any part of the body can activate that part of the body. Through concentration, even a paralyzed part can be cured. This is how biofeedback works. Biofeedback is based on concentration. Suppose something happens to this part, if I concentrate on this part, there will be good blood flow. Concentration can cure blocked arteries. Blocked arteries can be created by your bad breathing, shallow breathing. Coronary heart disease is related to shallow breathing. Westerners prefer short cuts. I am leading you through a short cut. But the shortest cut of all is to just cut your ego, nothing higher than that. To do that is very difficult.

Yoga teachers ask you to concentrate on the *ajna chakra*, eyebrow center, with breathing exercises, to increase your memory and intellect. For this is the gateway to the city of life. The teacher will give you concentration at the *vishuddha chakra*, throat center, if you are an artist, dancer, musician, or writer. If you are very emotional, the teacher will give you concentration at the *anahata chakra*, heart center. This chakra has two intersecting triangles, one upward and the other downward. Upward triangle indicates ascending power, that is, human effort. Downward triangle denotes descending power or grace. Where grace and human effort meet is called the Star of David, or anahata chakra. Those who are emotional can concentrate on this chakra and with the help of that emotional power they attain the higher state of ecstasy. Those who are not healthy will be advised to concentrate on the *manipura chakra,* navel center. Why? Because, close to the manipura chakra is the beginning of the biggest network of energy channels in the body, called *khanda,* a solar system, not just a fire place. The teacher will not allow you to meditate on the *swadhisthana chakra,* because, otherwise, the whole day you will be thinking of sex. With sexual diseases like frigidity and impotency, concentration on this chakra may be given.

Chapter 4
Stilling the Breath

"Controlling the breath, and thus calming the nerves, is a prerequisite to controlling the mind and the body."

Swami Rama

Prana is the first unit of energy and the vital energy of the universe. The whole universe is derived from *akasha* (space or ether) through prana. All the energies of the cosmos, of the sun, stars and all the galaxies, of thunder and lightning, of the wind and waves, of hurricanes, earthquakes and tsunamis are all manifestations of prana. The breath is the vehicle for prana.

Control of Breath	→	Control of Lungs
Control of Lungs	→	Control of Heart
Control of Heart	→	Control of Vagus Nerve
Control of Vagus Nerve	→	Control of ANS (Autonomic Nervous System)
Control of ANS	→	Control of Prana
Control of Prana	→	Control of Mind

As the breath can be voluntary or involuntary, it is an easy portal of entry for control of the autonomic nervous system and mind. Breath and mind are two sides of the same coin. There is reciprocity between breath and mind. If mind is disturbed, the breath is disturbed. If the breath is made calm, the mind becomes calm. Breath links body and mind and registers activity of both body and mind.

Breathing should be diaphragmatic not thoracic or clavicular. The breath should be:

Deep and complete (no shallowness)
Smooth (no jerks)
Silent (no noise)
Without a pause between inhalation and exhalation.

Diaphragmatic Breathing

The Diaphragm

The diaphragm is a large, dome-shaped sheet of muscle that separates the thoracic cavity from the abdominal cavity. During inhalation, it contracts and flattens, creating a vacuum in the thoracic cavity, thus expanding the lungs. During exhalation, it relaxes into the dome-shaped configuration, reducing the volume of the thoracic cavity and helping to empty the lungs (Figure 16).

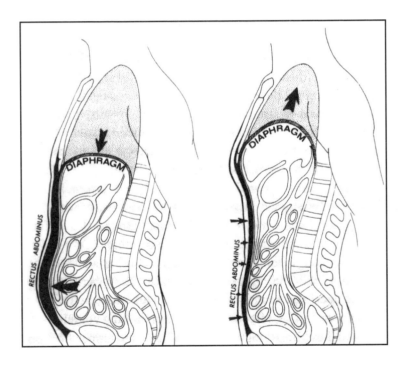

Figure 16

Advantages of Diaphragmatic Breathing

- Increases stroke volume and reduces respiration rate
- Increases efficiency of gas transfer in lungs
- Improves coronary circulation
- Reduces heart rate and load on the heart
- Lowers blood pressure
- Stimulates the lymphatic circulation
- Massages the abdominal organs
- Reduces sympathetic tone
- Increases parasympathetic tone
- Body becomes relaxed, mind becomes calm
- It is therapeutic for anxiety states

Practicum 1: Diaphragmatic Breathing

Although breathing is one of our most vital functions, it is little understood and often done improperly. Most people breathe in a shallow and haphazard manner, going against the natural rhythmic movement of the body's respiratory system. Diaphragmatic breathing, on the other hand, promotes a natural, even movement of breath that strengthens the nervous system and relaxes the body.

The principal muscle of diaphragmatic breathing, the diaphragm, is a strong, dome-shaped muscle. It divides the thoracic cavity, which contains the heart and lungs, from the abdominal cavity, which contains the organs of digestion, reproduction, and excretion. The diaphragm is located approximately two finger-widths below the nipples in its relaxed or dome-shaped state. It comes up slightly higher on the right side (between the fourth and fifth ribs) than it does on the left side (between the fifth and sixth ribs). In the center the diaphragm is located at the xiphoid process, the lower part of the sternum. The rectus abdominus, the two strong vertical muscles of the abdomen, work in cooperation with the diaphragm during diaphragmatic breathing.

During inhalation the diaphragm contracts and flattens; it pushes downward, causing the upper abdominal muscles to relax and extend slightly and the lower "floating" ribs to flare slightly outward. In this position the lungs expand, creating a partial vacuum, which draws air into the chest cavity. During exhalation the diaphragm relaxes and returns to its dome-shaped position. During this upward movement the upper abdominal muscles contract and air laden with carbon dioxide is forced out of the lungs.

Diaphragmatic breathing has three important effects on the body:

1. In diaphragmatic breathing, unlike shallow breathing, the lungs fill completely, providing the body with sufficient oxygen.

2. Diaphragmatic breathing forces the waste product of the respiratory process, carbon dioxide, from the lungs. With shallow breathing, some carbon dioxide may remain trapped in the lungs, causing fatigue and nervousness.

3. The up and down motion of the diaphragm gently massages the abdominal organs; this increases circulation to these organs and thus aids in their functioning.

In diaphragmatic breathing a minimum amount of effort is used to receive a maximum amount of air; thus, it is our most efficient method of breathing.

Technique

Note: Beginners should first learn diaphragmatic breathing in the crocodile posture described in Chapter 3. Having understood the basics of diaphragmatic breathing, they can continue the practice in the corpse posture as below:

Lie on the back with the feet a comfortable distance apart. Gently close the eyes and place one hand at the base of the rib cage and the other on the chest.

Inhale and exhale through the nostrils slowly, smoothly, and evenly, with no noise, jerks, or pauses in the breath. While inhaling, be aware of the upper abdominal muscles expanding and the lower ribs flaring out slightly. There should be little or no movement of the chest. Practice this method of deep breathing three to five minutes daily, until you clearly understand the movement of the diaphragm and the upper abdominal muscles. The body is designed to breathe diaphragmatically as is clearly observed in a newborn infant. It should again become natural and spontaneous.

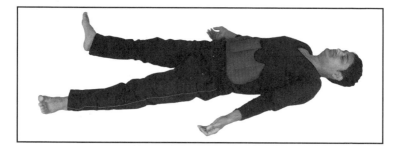

Figure 17

Sandbag Breathing

Just as dumbbells can be used to strengthen the muscles of the arms, a sandbag weighing 5 to 10 pounds can be used to strengthen the diaphragm and to perfect diaphragmatic breathing. The practice is done in shavasana and the sandbag is placed between the chest and the abdomen (Figure 17). During inhalation, as the diaphragm contracts and flattens, the abdominal wall has to rise moving the sandbag upward. During exhalation, the weight of the sandbag facilitates the descent of the abdominal wall and the diaphragm resumes its relaxed dome shape, emptying the lungs completely.

Practicum 2: Two to One Breathing

This is called an emergency breathing exercise. You can do it anywhere, on a plane too, but you have to be still while doing it. It is best to do it while sitting or lying down in shavasana. Don't do it while standing; you might fall.

So lie down in shavasana. Always use a thin pillow, otherwise, the upward movement of gastric gases, (apana vayu), may create a disturbance. Lie down in shavasana. Gently close your eyes and physically relax all your limbs, systematically moving upwards from the toes to your head and then coming down, physically relaxing. Start breathing diaphragmatically. Then let your mind follow the breath. The easiest way of concentrating the mind is to let the mind flow with the breath. Mind is very close to breath, but mind is not sincere to the breath. Through breath, you should learn to approach your mind, for mind and breath are twin laws of life. For a few minutes do diaphragmatic breathing, this is very helpful. That should become a habit.

The diaphragm is the strongest muscle in your body. With the help of it, you can even lift a grand piano. Its flexibility is lost if we do not do diaphragmatic breathing. As you exhale, push in your abdomen; then let it come out gently as you inhale. Don't exert yourself when you are releasing your muscle, only use your effort when you are exhaling, pushing in. If you are not doing this, you will not be able to inhale as much as you can. You can eliminate any situation of your mind, any sorrow, any sadness, by this type of breathing. Whenever you are sad, just breathe deeply and you are free. Whenever you are going through any emotional problem just breathe deeply and you are free. You are accumulating toxins inside, and these toxins are injurious to your whole being, that's why you are miserable. You should not allow toxins to build up in your body. You build up these toxins through food, through breath, and through thinking.

Try to relax your limbs and muscles as much as you can. First you have to exhale, that's called *rechaka*. Let your mind flow with your breath, because they are the greatest friends in the world. No one can attain as good a friendship as mind and breath. If mind wants to distract breath, breath is always distracted; you will not be healthy. If breath is calm, it can help to make your mind calm. Now you are allowing your mind to flow with the breath, as you exhale. When you go beyond your capacity in exhalation, there will be a jerk. You have to watch your capacity. So you should work with the digital system. First you can use a ratio of 8 to 4, exhalation to a count of 8 and inhalation to a count of 4. This is just the starting ratio. Later, it can be increased. Any respiratory problem or any emotional problem can be nipped by this method; it's very therapeutic for the mind and for the breath. It's very good for the heart, nervous system, and brain. Your memory will improve if you follow this method. The ratio of 8:4, 8 counts exhalation and 4 counts inhalation, can be used in cloth mills, mines and other polluted places, where you find particles getting into your lungs. When your lungs are being polluted by such particles, practice this type of breathing two to three times a day, five minutes at a time. When you inhale it goes to your storehouse, the lungs, and when you exhale you are forcing toxins like carbon dioxide from your lungs and all the muscles in which toxins are distributed. You are forcing your whole system, lungs and all muscles to release carbon dioxide and you are inhaling to your full capacity. This is very healthy.

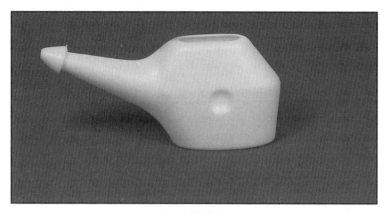

Figure 18

Neti

The functions of the nasal passages include filtering, moisturizing, warming, directing airflow, sense of smell, drainage of sinuses, producing mucus and signaling the autonomic nervous system. It is, therefore, very important to keep the nasal passages clean and open. Neti, or nasal wash is a yogic technique to clean the nasal passage and help drain the sinuses.

Jala Neti: Nasal Wash with Salt Water

A neti pot (Figure 18) with a suitable spout is used for the nasal wash. The neti pot is filled with lukewarm salty water, the saltiness being about the same as one's tears. With the head tilted to the side and forward, the spout of the neti pot is inserted into one of the nostrils and the salty water is allowed to flow by gravity through that nostril, around, and out through the other nostril (Figure 19). The process is then reversed with the spout placed in the other nostril. After emptying the neti pot, blow out any residual water through both nostrils. With practice, the tilt of the

Figure 19

head can also be adjusted to drain the salty water out of the mouth rather than the other nostril. This helps completely clean the respiratory passages. The salty water not only drains away the accumulated mucus and filtered dirt, but it also causes the swollen nasal passages and turbinates to shrink due to osmosis. Drainage of the sinuses is thus facilitated. If practiced daily, sinus congestion is prevented. Also allergens like pollen are washed away, making one less prone to upper respiratory inflammation and infections.

Sutra Neti: String Neti

Instead of cleansing the respiratory passages with water, a string with a wax-stiffened end or a rubber catheter can be used (Figure 20). The catheter is inserted into one nostril and gently advanced till it comes out at the back of the throat. This end is then caught hold of, and the catheter gently milked to and fro, massaging and cleaning the respiratory passage (Figure 21). The process is then repeated

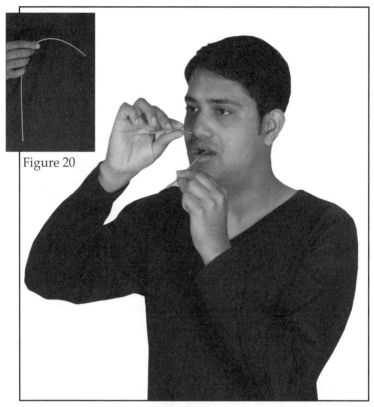

Figure 21

with the other nostril. The practice of *sutra neti* strengthens the mucus membranes lining the respiratory passages and is also beneficial for the eyes.

Practicum 3: Nadi Shodhanam (Alternate Nostril Breathing)

Nadi shodhanam restores balance between the ida and pingala nadis. It also cleanses and strengthens the nervous system. It restores balance between the sympathetic and parasympathetic divisions of the autonomic nervous system. This kriya is preliminary to opening up and energizing sushumna. Sushumna energization is preliminary to awakening the sleeping *kundalini shakti* at the base of the spine.

Nostril Dominance

The nasal passages are lined with erectile tissue. Blood engorgement swells this tissue and alters airflow. Nostril dominance alternates approximately every two hours. The right nostril is called the solar nostril. Activation of this nostril is heat producing and gears the body up for activity through activation of the sympathetic nervous system. The left nostril is called the lunar nostril. Activation of this nostril is cooling and produces relaxation by activating the parasympathetic nervous system.

Problems with Single Nostril Dominance

Normally nostril dominance changes every 100 to 120 minutes. It is not good to have one nostril dominant all the time. If the right nostril stays dominant all the time, it results in anger, hyperactivity, aggression and hypertension.

If the left nostril stays dominant all the time, it results in depression, fatigue, weak digestion and sleepiness.

Nadi Shodhanam: Variation 1

The practice of nadi shodhanam or alternate nostril breathing should be done in a seated position with the head, neck and trunk erect and aligned. The exercise should be done at least twice a day, at dawn and dusk, when the solar and lunar energies are in conjunction and balanced. This balancing of the macrocosmic energies facilitates the balancing of the microcosmic solar and lunar energies, that is, the flow of breath through the right (solar) and left (lunar) nostrils. One should choose a calm, quiet and well-ventilated place for the practice. As the nostrils need to be alternately closed and opened, a special mudra called the

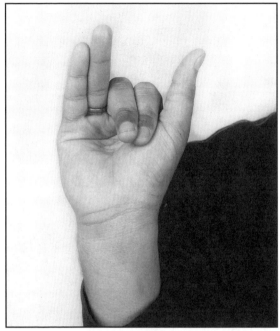

Figure 22A

Vishnu mudra (Figure 22A) is used. In this mudra, the index and middle fingers of the right hand are folded, the right thumb being used for closing the right nostril and the right ring finger being used to close the left nostril Figure 22B).

- One starts the practice by inhaling slowly and deeply through both nostrils. At dawn, as the sun is rising, one starts exhaling through the lunar or left nostril, keeping the right nostril closed. (At dusk, the first exhalation is through the right nostril to balance the rising lunar energy.) After a complete exhalation through the left nostril, the left nostril is closed with the thumb and one inhales slowly and deeply through the right nostril. This is breath 1 of the round. This process is repeated with breaths 2 and 3.

Figure 22B

- At the end of the third inhalation through the right nostril, the left nostril remains closed with the ring finger and exhalation is through the right nostril followed by inhalation through the left nostril. Thus with breath 4, there is a switch of the nostrils in terms of exhalation and inhalation. Breaths 5 and 6 are the same as breath 4, namely exhalation through the right nostril and inhalation through the left nostril.
- After these 6 breaths, the hand is lowered and rested on the knees while three cleansing breaths are taken through both nostrils thus completing the first round of nadi shodhanam.
- To summarize, Variation 1, at dawn, consists of 3 exhalations through the left nostril with the

inhalations being through the right nostril, followed by 3 exhalations through the right nostril with inhalations through the left nostril. The round is completed with 3 cleansing breaths through both nostrils.

- To start with, one should practice 3 rounds at each sitting, at dawn and dusk. At dawn, the first round starts with exhalation through the left nostril and inhalation through the right nostril. The second round starts with exhalation through the right nostril and inhalation through the left nostril. The third round is the same as the first round.

- The number of rounds at each sitting can be increased to 10 rounds. If time permits, even more rounds can be added. As another option, the number of sittings can be increased to 3 a day, at dawn, noon and dusk.

Nadi Shodhanam: Variation 2

Variation 2 also consists of 6 breaths followed by 3 cleansing breaths. However, at dawn, the first 3 exhalations and inhalations are through the left nostril, the right remaining closed through all 3 breaths. Then the breathing switches to the right nostril and for breaths 4, 5 and 6, exhalation and inhalation are through the right nostril only, the left remaining closed. After this, the hands are lowered and 3 cleansing breaths are taken through both nostrils

Nadi Shodhanam: Variation 3

Variation 3 also consists of 6 breaths followed by 3 cleansing breaths. However, at dawn, the first exhalation and inhalation are through the left nostril, the right remaining closed. Then the breathing switches to the right nostril, and breath 2 consists of exhalation and inhalation through the right nostril only, the left remaining closed. Breaths 3 and 5 are the same as breath 1. Breaths 4 and 6 are the same as breath 2. After this, the hands are lowered and three cleansing breaths are taken through both nostrils. To summarize, breaths 1, 3 and 5 are exhalations and inhalations through the left nostril, while breaths 2, 4 and 6 are exhalations and inhalations through the right nostril. The round closes with the 3 cleansing breaths through booth nostrils.

Practicum 4: Sushumna Application

For success in meditation, you have to establish tranquility and achieve a joyous mind *(sukha manah)*. And for that, the system is to apply sushumna, a simple method of breath awareness. To begin the process of sushumna awakening, ask your mind to focus on the space between the two nostrils, where the upper lip meets the nostrils. Focus the mind on the breath as it flows past this point, the flow being equally through both nostrils. This first step in learning sushumna application is learning to change the flow of your breath with your mind. To accomplish this process you must learn to create a relaxed focus on the blocked nostril. When the mind focuses on the blocked nostril, it will become active. When you have learned to mentally change the flow of the breath in the nostrils, then a time comes, when you can make the breath flow evenly through both nostrils. This may take some months or even a year, depending on your capacity and the burning desire within you. When both nostrils flow freely, that is called *sandhya,* the wedding of the sun and moon, that is of the ida and pingala nadis. Once this experience can be maintained for five minutes, the student has crossed a great barrier, the mind has attained one-pointedness and becomes inward-focused. When the nostrils flow evenly, the mind cannot worry because it is disconnected from the senses. Then, mind attains a state of joy that is conducive to deep meditation.

Some Basic Exercises of Pranayama

Kapalabhati

Kapalabhati, in Sanskrit, means that which makes the skull *(kapala)* shine *(bhati).* Strictly speaking, it is not an exercise of pranayama but one of the *shat* (six) *kriyas,* the six cleansing processes of Hatha Yoga. The shat kriyas are neti (cleansing of the nostrils), *dhauti,* (cleansing the stomach of mucus), *nauli* (cleansing of the digestive system by manipulation of the rectus abdominis muscles), *basti* (cleansing of the colon), kapalabhati (cleansing of the respiratory passages and sinuses), and *trataka* (gazing techniques to strengthen the eyes and develop concentration). Kapalabhati is a breathing exercise rather than an exercise of pranayama. It not only cleans the respiratory passages and sinuses but, more importantly, it cleanses the nadis or pranic channels.

Kapalabhati should be done in a seated position. If one can sit cross-legged, then siddhasana (or the adept's posture) with foot lock is most suitable. Because of the vigor of the exhalation, there is a tendency for the vigorous jerks to make the body shake making the posture unstable. Siddhasana with the foot lock or the lotus posture are recommended for kapalabhati. If one cannot sit on the ground, kapalabhati may be practiced sitting on a chair but with head, neck and trunk in a straight line and with the feet firmly planted on the floor or on a cushion resting on the floor.

In normal respiration, inhalation is an active process and exhalation is passive. In kapalabhati, exhalation is active and forceful, while inhalation is a passive filling of the lungs after the forceful exhalation. The abdominal muscles are contracted vigorously and the diaphragm becomes rapidly dome-shaped during the forceful exhalation. During inhalation, the abdominal muscles pull the diaphragm down into a flat configuration. The duration of the inhalation is about four times the duration of the exhalation. There is no pause or holding of the breath between exhalation and inhalation.

To start with, one can do 11 exhalations and inhalations in one round followed by a half to one minute of normal deep diaphragmatic breathing. Three rounds can be done at each sitting with two sittings (morning and evening) each day. The number of exhalations (and inhalations) in each round can be gradually increased to a maximum of 120. Traditionally, each week, the number of breaths in a round can be doubled till 120 breaths are reached. If one starts with 11 breaths per round, then it will take approximately four weeks to reach the target of 120 breaths per round. In the beginning, the speed or rate of breaths can be one breath per second. Gradually, the rate can be increased to two breaths per second, or 120 breaths in one minute. More important than the rate (or speed) is the vigor of the exhalation. Vigor should not be sacrificed for speed. However, one's general health and capacity should be taken into consideration and the number increased judiciously. It should not be forgotten that ahimsa, or non-violence is one of the major guiding principles (one of the five yamas) of yoga.

Kapalabhati improves oxygenation of the blood and tissues as well as removal of carbon dioxide from the tissues and blood. Kapalabhati also provides vigorous massage of the abdominal viscera. It helps prevent respiratory ailments and can arrest the aging process. The nervous system is strengthened and the circulation and metabolism improve. From the perspective of spiritual sadhana, the practice of kapalabhati will cleanse the nadis and stimulate the energy centers. Kapalabhati is preliminary to practicing the more advanced techniques of pranayama.

Bhastrika

Bhastrika is one of the exercises of pranayama. Bhastrika, in Sanskrit, means bellows. The rapid and forceful exhalations and inhalations of bhastrika produce movements (of the chest and abdomen) and sounds reminiscent of a blacksmith working the bellows of his furnace.

Bhastrika is practiced in a stable sitting posture as in the case of kapalabhati. While, in kapalabhati only the exhalation is forceful and inhalation is passive, in bhastrika, both exhalation and inhalation are forceful and rapid, without retention of the breath in between. Both nostrils are used for forceful exhalation and inhalation and there is more movement of the chest compared to kapalabhati, where the focus is on vigorous contraction of the abdominal muscles.

Bhastrika starts with a deep inhalation followed by a rapid succession of exhalations and inhalations. To start with one can do between 7 and 21 rapid exhalations and inhalations.

Variations of Bhastrika

There are three variations of bhastrika pranayama. In the first variation, the front bellows, the forced rapid exhalations and inhalations are done with both nostrils open and with the face looking forward. Between rounds, deep diaphragmatic breathing through both nostrils is done for a half to one minute.

In the second variation, the side to side bellows, the first burst of exhalation and inhalation is done with the head facing the front. For the second rapid breath, the head is turned to the right (in the morning, but in the evening, the head is turned to the left). For the third breath, the head returns to the middle, to the left for the fourth breath, back to the middle for the fifth breath and so on, till the desired number of rapid breaths for the round is achieved. The second round can be done by turning from the middle to the left (in the morning) rather than to the right for the second breath, middle for the third, right for the fourth, middle for the fifth and so on. The third round is exactly the same as the first round.

In the third variation, the alternate nostril bellows, there is alternation of the nostrils after each rapid exhalation and inhalation. To make it clearer, the first rapid exhalation and inhalation is done through the right nostril. The second rapid exhalation and inhalation is through the left nostril, the third being through the right and so on. The thumb is used to close the right nostril while the middle and ring fingers are used to close the left nostril with the Vishnu mudra. In this variation, the second round of bhastrika, can start with the left nostril. The third round is exactly the same as the first round.

Ujjayi

This pranayama is also done seated in a stable posture with the head, neck and trunk aligned and erect. Start by exhaling completely. The inhalation is done with the abdominal muscles slightly contracted and with a partially closed glottis, making a soft, continuous sound accompanied by the sibilant sound "sa," like sobbing. The incoming air is felt on the roof of the palate. Without any pause, the exhalation is also done with a partially closed glottis, exerting abdominal pressure till all of the air is exhaled accompanied by the aspirant sound "ha." The outgoing air is again felt on the roof of the palate. This completes one cycle of *ujjayi* and the pranayama can be practiced for about three to five minutes. This pranayama clears the nasal passages of phlegm, soothes the nervous system and calms the mind.

Brahmari

In Sanskrit, *brahmari* means a bee. The pranayama is so called because the sound made during exhalation resembles the humming sound of a bee. Inhale deeply through both nostrils and while exhaling, make a humming sound. Repeat with several breaths and feel the humming vibration at the throat, in the whole cranium and spreading out through the body. This will soothe the nervous system and calm the restless mind. This is a simple exercise that even young children can learn. It will help calm them down and they will enjoy doing the pranayama.

Chapter 5
Stilling the Senses and Mind
through Relaxation

"In Yoga, the body has to follow the mind not vice versa." These exercises train the body and mind together. They exercise the unconscious mind and lead the practitioner to a state of mind where it is possible to consciously control the involuntary nervous system. To relax completely, the technique of relaxation should be systematic and progressive involving the muscles, joints, breath, nervous system and mind. Such complete relaxation lowers blood pressure, reduces the heart and respiration rate and lowers the basal metabolic rate. Improvements in cognition and memory are also experienced.

Kriya 1: Relaxation (Muscles and Joints)
This kriya is done in shavasana, using a thin pillow under the head and neck and with a dark-colored (red/black) handkerchief over the eyes.

4 exhalations and inhalations
Head and face:
Relax the top of the head, forehead, eyebrows, eyelids and
  nostrils.
2 exhalations and inhalations

Jaw, neck, shoulders and arms:
Relax the mouth, jaw, chin, neck, shoulders, upper arms,
  lower arms, palms, fingers, finger tips.
2 exhalations and inhalations

Arms, shoulders and chest:
Relax the fingers, palms, lower arms, upper arms, shoulders, neck and chest.
4 exhalations and inhalations
Exhale all strain, burnt residues of all body cells, carbon dioxide. Inhale vitality, energy, strength and fresh oxygen.

Stomach, pelvis, legs and feet:
Relax the stomach, lower abdomen, pelvis, hips, thighs, calf muscles, feet and toes.
4 exhalations and inhalations

Leg joints, hips, pelvis and stomach:
Relax the toe joints, ankle joints, knees, hip joints, pelvis, lower abdomen and navel.

Chest, shoulders and arms:
Relax the cardiac center, throat center, shoulder joints, elbows, wrists and finger joints.
2 exhalations and inhalations

Hands, shoulders, throat:
Relax the joints of the fingers, wrists, elbows, shoulder joints, throat center, neck and jaws.
Head and face:
Relax the mouth, nostrils, eyelids, eyebrows, forehead, and top of the head.

Kriya 2A:
Beginning Tense - Relax Exercise, in Shavasana
This kriya is done in shavasana, using a thin pillow under the head and neck and with a dark-colored (red/black) handkerchief over the eyes.

Tense the face; pull the muscles toward the tip of the nose; relax the face completely.

Close your eyes and roll your head from one side to the other, on the floor.

Pull the shoulders forward; release the tension and relax.

Tense the right arm on the floor; release the tension and relax. Do the same with the left arm.

Tense the hips and the buttocks; let go of the tension and relax.

Tense the right leg; relax. Do the same with the left leg.

Relax the toes, legs, thighs, hips, back, chest, arms, shoulders, neck, face and head.

Note: It is important to continue to breathe while tensing the body. Do not hold the breath.

Kriya 2B: Intermediate Tense - Relax Exercise

This kriya is done in shavasana, using a thin pillow under the head and neck and with a dark-colored (red/ black) handkerchief over the eyes.

Relax the whole body with four deep exhalations and inhalations.

Tense the left arm by turning the palm downward and pressing against the floor.

Right arm is relaxed.

Relax the left arm.

Tense the right arm by turning the palm downward and pressing against the floor.

Relax the right arm.

Now tense both arms, the rest of the body being relaxed.

Now relax both arms.

Tense the right arm and left leg keeping the left arm and right leg relaxed.

Tense the leg by stretching the leg and pointing the toes away from the body.

Relax the right arm and left leg.

Tense the left arm and right leg keeping the right arm and left leg relaxed.

Tense the leg by stretching the leg and pointing the toes away from the body.

Relax the left arm and right leg.

Tense the upper part of the body keeping the lower part relaxed.

Relax the upper part of the body.

Tense the lower part of the body keeping the upper part relaxed.

Relax the lower part of the body.

Kriya 2C: Advanced Tense - Relax Exercise

This kriya is done in shavasana, using a thin pillow under the head and neck and with a dark-colored (red/ black) handkerchief over the eyes.

Preparation

The stomach should be empty of food (allow at least two and a half hours after eating). Go to the bathroom and empty the bladder (also bowels if possible). Shower or do *pancha snana* (washing your hands, face, and feet). The room should be made dark; no phones or other potential disturbance. Sudden noises should be avoided. It is important to choose a time when there will be no interruptions. Arrange a blanket or mat on the floor with a thin pillow to support your head. Cover yourself with a light blanket or shawl to shield your body from drafts.

The Practice

Position yourself in shavasana with feet apart but with the palms of your hands on the floor. In this exercise, there is conscious tensing of various parts of the body in a definite sequence, followed by a conscious relaxation of the same part of the body. Tensing is done during inhalation imagining an ascending wave counting off each second thus: 1001, 1002, 1003, 1004. . . . This is followed by relaxation with exhalation, imagining a descending wave, again counting off the seconds as before.

Start the practice by taking 10 relaxing full body breaths, inhaling from the toes to the head, and exhaling from the head to the toes. The muscles of your face should remain relaxed, no grimacing or other expressions. Maintain relaxation in all parts of the body. Starting with the right hand, press the fingertip of the little finger against the floor, tensing and stretching the little finger only. Do this as you are inhaling (tense 1001, 1002, 1003, etc.) Then relax from the base of the finger down to the tip, with exhalation (relax 1001, 1002, 1003, etc.). Proceed to the ring finger and repeat the same process, but with only the ring finger tensed and all the other fingers relaxed and not engaged in the exercise. Also, check to make sure that you are not creating or holding tension in any other area of the body.

Continue the same process of tensing and relaxing with the middle finger, index finger and thumb. Give each digit its individual attention. Maintain smoothness of breath. Do not hold the breath at any time. When you have finished relaxing the thumb, press all five fingertips against the floor. Stretch and tense the fingers. Stretch and tense the wrist joint. Stretch and tense the elbow. Stretch and tense the shoulder joint.

All of this is done in a kind of ascending wave of tension up the arm from the fingertips to the shoulder joint, while inhaling and counting. Then exhale and release the tension starting from the shoulder joint in a descending wave of relaxation down to the fingertips while counting. Take three relaxing whole body breaths.

Then, repeat the sequence with the fingers of the left hand starting with the little finger and continuing as before from the fingers to the shoulder joint. Always check the rest of your body to be sure that all other muscles are relaxed.

When finished with the left arm, take three whole body relaxing breaths.

The next step is to work with both arms at the same time.

Press all 10 fingers against the floor, stretching and tensing first the fingers, then tensing and stretching at the wrists, elbows, and shoulder joints as you count while inhaling in an ascending wave.

Exhale and release the tension in both arms, starting with the shoulder joints and working down to the fingertips in a descending wave of relaxation, with counting as before. Be sure to check that you are not clenching your jaw, or tensing any other part of your body. Everything else should remain relaxed, while giving attention to the specific area being exercised.

When tension is released from both arms, take three whole body relaxing breaths.

Now, start with the legs. Starting with the right foot, tense and relax the little toe with inhalation and exhalation. Work each toe in turn, just as you did with the fingers, till you get to the big toe.

Note: Other than your big toe and possibly the second toe, you may have no clue as to how to become aware of each toe, individually. One way to help develop "toe awareness" is to use your fingers. This is done at some other time, not during the exercise. Reach down to your foot, and place the tip of a finger under each of the four toes, one toe at a time. You need not do this with the big toe, which of course you can wiggle. While pressing with the finger, try to press the finger back with the toe. This way you can make a mental connection of "toe awareness." Anything that could not be done physically (in this exercise), should be done mentally (in the mind's imaging).

When you have completed the tension and relaxation sequence with the individual toes, proceed to work with the whole right leg thus:

Tense and stretch all five toes.
Tense and stretch from the ankle.
Tense and stretch from the knee.
Tense and stretch from the hip.

All of the above is done in an ascending wave, tensing and stretching from the joints as you are inhaling and counting (1001, 1002, 1003, etc.). Then exhaling and release the tension in a descending wave starting with the hip and ending with the toes while counting (1001, 1002, 1003, etc.).

At the end of this sequence take three whole body relaxing breaths.

Repeat the sequence with the toes of the left foot (starting with the little toe) and follow by working with the left leg as with the right leg.

When finished with the left leg and toes, take three whole body relaxing breaths.

The next step is to work with both legs at the same time. Tense and stretch all 10 toes and in an ascending wave, tense and stretch from the ankles, knees, and hips while smoothly inhaling and counting. Release tension from the hips and in a descending wave down both legs to the toes, exhaling smoothly and counting.

At the end of this sequence take three whole body relaxing breaths.

Now bring your attention to the base of your spinal column. There are a total of 32 vertebrae. You have to focus on each vertebra, one at a time , from #1 at the base of the spine to #32 at the back of the skull. You are to breathe in and out (one breath) through each vertebra. When you have completed the focus on vertebra #32, take three relaxing whole body breaths.

Note: To help with the focus on the 32 vertebrae, you may consult a high quality anatomical chart of the spinal column. The first thing you will notice is that all vertebrae are not the same size, for correct postural orientation. You can take the help of a friend to learn where each vertebrae is positioned in your body. Internally, it helps to visualize each vertebrae bathed in light as you bring your mental focus to it. Remember to inhale and exhale through each vertebra (32 vertebrae = 32 breaths).

The final step: While inhaling smoothly, tense and stretch all 10 fingers and all 10 toes.

Stretch and tense in an ascending wave, up both arms and both legs, all four extremities at the same time. When you come to the hips, proceed to tense (lengthen and stretch) from the base of the spine up to the head. Keep the face relaxed; otherwise it is a whole body stretch. Exhaling, release the tension in a descending wave, down the spine and down both arms and both legs, all at the same time. When all tension has been released, take 10 deep smooth breaths, as though the whole body is expanding with each inhalation and the whole body is contracting with each exhalation.

The tense–relax kriya can be done on its own. However, you are encouraged to make it part of a regular morning routine, to precede your sitting for meditation. You will need to start at least one hour before your scheduled time for meditation. Build the practice gradually. If you wake up 15 minutes earlier than your usual time, and work with one of the practices, your body will not notice the difference of 15 minutes less sleep. After two to three weeks, take off another 15 minutes of sleep time. Working this way with yourself, you can replace sleep time with practice time in a gentle way that your body and mind will accept. Your first reaction may be that you do not have enough time in your busy life for such a practice. Carefully examine your desires and priorities. If you sincerely want to do it, you will make the time.

Summary of the Sequence for the Advanced Tense-Relax Kriya

1. 10 relaxing whole body breaths
2. Tense-relax fingers of right hand to shoulder
3. 3 relaxing whole body breaths
4. Tense-relax fingers of left hand to shoulder
5. 3 relaxing whole body breaths
6. Tense-relax both arms
7. 3 relaxing whole body breaths
8. Tense-relax toes of right leg to hip
9. 3 relaxing whole body breaths
10. Tense-relax toes of left leg to hip
11. 3 relaxing whole body breaths
12. Tense-relax both legs
13. 3 relaxing whole body breaths
14. 32 vertebrae breaths
15. 3 relaxing whole body breaths
16. Tense-relax whole body
17. 10 relaxing whole body breaths

Kriya 3: Shavayatra (Traveling through the Body)

3A: 31 Point Exercise

This exercise is known as *shavayatra,* which means inner pilgrimage through the body. In this exercise awareness is directed and focused on 31 sacred points of the body (Figure

31 Point Exercise

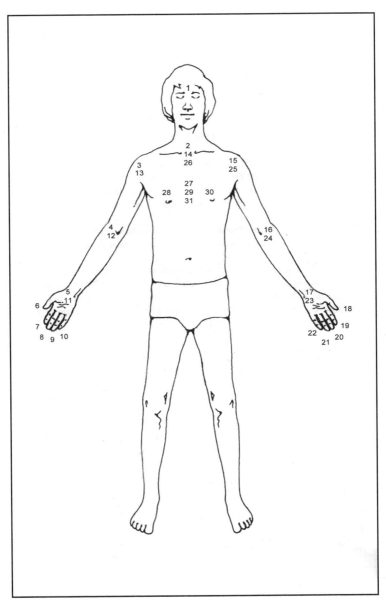

Figure 23

23). This allows the student to closely scan the body with the mind, inspecting the body to discover where problems lie.

Lie in the corpse posture or shavasana, with a thin pillow supporting your head and with a dark-colored (red/black) handkerchief over the eyes.

Become aware of your breathing. Breathe deeply, smoothly and evenly, without any pauses or noise.

Starting with the top of your head, relax your head and face. Relax your neck and shoulders. Relax the upper arms, lower arms, palms and fingers.

Relax your finger joints, wrists, elbows, shoulder joints and neck.

Relax your chest, navel, lower abdomen and hips.

Relax your thighs, calves, feet and toes.

Relax your toe joints, ankles, knees and hip joints. Relax the whole pelvis.

Relax your chest, shoulders and neck. Relax the face and head.

Continue to breathe deeply, smoothly and evenly without pauses or noise.

In this exercise you will pay attention, sequentially to 31 special points of the body, as shown in Figure 23.

Now, bring your attention to the space between the eyebrows, the eyebrow center.

Keep your attention at this point and think of the number "1."

We will now proceed through the remaining 30 points of this exercise.

Bring your awareness to the center of your throat, 2.

Right shoulder joint, 3.

Right elbow joint, 4.

Right wrist joint, 5.

Tip of the right thumb, 6.

Tip of the right index finger, 7.

Tip of the right middle finger, 8.

Tip of the right ring finger, 9.

Tip of the right little finger, 10.

Now back up to the right wrist joint, 11.

Right elbow joint, 12.

Right shoulder joint, 13.

Bring your awareness to the center of your throat, 14.

Now go across to the left shoulder joint, 15.

Left elbow joint, 16.

Left wrist joint, 17.

Tip of the left thumb, 18.

Tip of the left index finger, 19.

Tip of the left middle finger, 20.

Tip of the left ring finger, 21.

Tip of the little finger of the left hand, 22.

Back up to the left wrist joint, 23.

Left elbow joint, 24.

Left shoulder joint, 25.

Bring your awareness to the center of the throat, 26.

Now bring your awareness down to the center between the two breasts, 27.

Now across to the right side of the chest, 28.

Back to the center between the two breasts, 29.

Across to the left side of the chest, 30.

And finally back to the center between the two breasts, 31.

This concludes the 31 point exercise.

Continue to breathe deeply, smoothly and evenly, without any pauses or noise.

After you have practiced this exercise for seven to ten days with numbers, you can visualize a blue light or a golden light at each of the 31 points, instead of the numbers.

When this exercise can be done without the mind wandering, you are ready for the 61 point exercise.

OM, shanti, shanti, shantihi. OM, peace, peace, peace.

3B: 61 Point Exercise

When the 31 point exercise can be done without allowing the mind to wander, then you are ready for the 61 point exercise. The 61 points are shown in Figure 24. Practice the 61 point exercise after relaxation and before pranayama (breathing exercises). The exercise may be begun on either the right or left side, but be consistent. If you begin (on the torso) with the right arm, then in the lower extremities also begin with the right leg. The 61 point exercise should not be practiced when you feel sleepy or tired.

61 Point Exercise

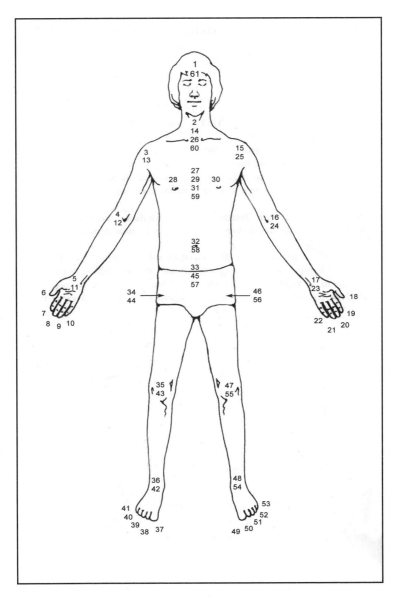

Figure 24

Lie in the corpse posture or shavasana, with a thin pillow supporting your head.

Become aware of your breathing.

Breathe deeply, smoothly and evenly, without any pauses or noise.

Starting with the top of your head, relax your head and face.

Relax your neck and shoulders.

Relax the upper arms, lower arms, palms and fingers.

Relax your finger joints, wrists, elbows, shoulder joints and neck.

Relax your chest, navel, lower abdomen and hips.

Relax your thighs, calves, feet and toes.

Relax your toe joints, ankles, knees and hip joints.

Relax the whole pelvis.

Relax your navel, chest, shoulders and neck.

Relax the face and head.

Continue to breathe deeply, smoothly and evenly without pauses or noise.

In this exercise you will pay attention, sequentially to 61 special points of the body.

Bring your attention to the space between the eyebrows, the eyebrow center.

Keep your attention at this point and think of the number "1."

We will now proceed through the remaining 60 special points of the body.

Bring your awareness to the hollow of your throat, 2.

Right shoulder joint, 3.

Right elbow joint, 4.

Right wrist joint, 5.

Tip of the right thumb, 6.

Tip of the right index finger, 7.

Tip of the right middle finger, 8.

Tip of the right ring finger, 9.

Tip of the right little finger, 10.

Now come back up to the right wrist joint, 11.

Right elbow joint, 12.

Right shoulder joint, 13.

Bring your awareness to the center of your throat, 14.

Now go across to the left shoulder joint, 15.

Left elbow joint, 16.

Left wrist joint, 17.

Tip of the left thumb, 18.

Tip of the left index finger, 19.

Tip of the left middle finger, 20.

Tip of the left ring finger, 21.

Tip of the little finger of the left hand, 22.

Back up to the left wrist joint, 23.

Left elbow joint, 24.

Left shoulder joint, 25.

Bring your awareness to the center of the throat, 26.

Now bring your awareness down to the center between the two breasts, 27.

Now across to the right side of the chest, 28.

Back to the center between the two breasts, 29.

Across to the left side of the chest, 30.

Again back to the center between the two breasts, 31.

Now bring your awareness down to the navel center, 32.

Come down to the pelvic center, 33.

Go across with your awareness to the right hip joint, 34.

Down to the right knee joint, 35.

Right ankle joint, 36.

Now bring your awareness to the big toe of the right foot, 37.

Second toe, 38.

Middle toe, 39.

Fourth toe, 40.

Little toe of the right foot, 41.

Now come up to the right ankle joint, 42.

Right knee joint, 43.

Right hip joint, 44.

Back to the pelvic center, 45.

Now go across to the left hip joint, 46.

Left knee joint, 47.

Left ankle joint, 48.

Bring your awareness to the big toe of the left foot, 49.

Second toe, 50.

Middle toe, 51.

Fourth toe, 52.

Little toe of the left foot, 53.

Now, come up to the left ankle joint, 54.

Left knee joint, 55.

Left hip joint, 56.

Come back to the pelvic center, 57.

Up to the navel center, 58.

Up further to the heart center at the center of the chest, 59.

Bring your awareness to the throat center, 60.

Come up to the eyebrow center, 61.

Continue to breathe deeply, smoothly, evenly and without a pause or noise for a few minutes.

Feel as if you are breathing out and in through the eyebrow center.

This concludes the 61 point exercise.

OM, shanti, shanti, shantihi.

OM, peace, peace, peace.

Notes on the 31 / 61 Point Exercise:

These two exercises are subtle, yet profound exercises for getting access to the sheaths of prana (vitality) and mind. These exercises can help the aspirant detect regions of the body where there is some weakness or disturbance of pranic flow. Disturbances in the body are preceded by disturbances in the pranic flow, which are in turn preceded by disturbances in the mind. The mind will consistently wander off at the same point each time, indicating weakness around that point.

Scanning the body through the 31 point and 61 point exercises helps uncover the root cause of disturbances that manifest ultimately in the body. Such bodily disturbances can be preempted by dealing with these disturbances at the mental level. High blood pressure, high blood sugar, peptic and gastric ulcers, circulatory problems and stress can all be significantly alleviated by the regular practice of the 31 point/61 point exercise.

3C: 77 Point Exercise

Once the 61 point exercise has been mastered without the mind wandering away and losing track of the count, the 77 point exercise may be attempted (Figure 25). In this variation, one proceeds further from the eyebrow center (point 61) to the two petals of the eyebrow chakra (points 62 and 63), then to the throat center (point 64), on to the heart center (eight petals, points 65-73), and terminating the kriya at the upward triangle of the navel center (points 74-77). The kriya is completed by mentally chanting one's mantra eleven times at the navel center.

As a variation, in the 31, 61, and 77 point exercises, instead of counting the number at each point, visualize a blue star at each point and travel with the blue star from point to point. The blue star is your companion on the

77 Point Exercise

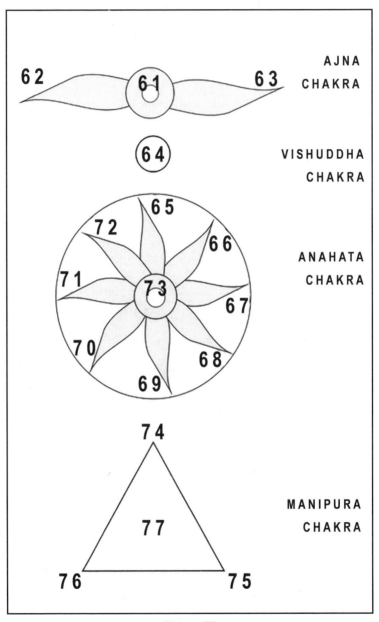

Figure 25

pilgrimage of the various holy places that you visit on this journey.

Kriya 4: Relaxation of Muscles, Joints and Chakras in Shavasana

This kriya is done in shavasana, using a thin pillow under the head and neck and with a dark-colored (red/ black) handkerchief over the eyes.

2 exhalations and inhalations
Head and face:
Relax the top of the head, forehead, eyebrows, eyelids, nostrils, mouth, corners of the mouth, cheeks and jaw.
4 exhalations and inhalations

Neck, shoulders and arms:
Relax the neck, right shoulder, right shoulder joint, right upper arm, right elbow, right forearm, right wrist, right palm, fingers, finger joints and finger tips. Move back up in reverse order to right shoulder.
Relax the neck, left shoulder, left shoulder joint, left upper arm, left elbow, left forearm, left wrist, left palm, fingers, finger joints and finger tips. Move back up in reverse order to left shoulder.
2 exhalations and inhalations

Cardiac plexus:
Relax the cardiac plexus, right breast, cardiac plexus, left breast. Visualize an upward triangle and an intersecting downward triangle filled with a pure white light. Feel this aura of purity, peace and brilliance.

Navel and abdomen:
Relax the navel muscles and lower abdomen.

Hips, legs and feet:

Relax the right hip, right hip joint, right thigh, right knee, right calf, right ankle, right foot, toe joints and toes. Move back up in the reverse order to the right hip.

Relax the left hip, left hip joint, left thigh, left knee, left calf, left ankle, left foot, toe joints and toes. Move back up in the reverse order to the left hip.

Relax downwards with an exhalation from the pelvis, hips, both thighs, both knees, both calves, both ankles, both feet and toes.

4 deep inhalations and exhalations from toes to eyebrows and back down to toes.

Relax the toes, feet, ankles, calves, knees, thighs, thigh joints and hips.

Chakras

Muladhara: Relax the base of the spine and visualize a slender streak of lightning, coiled around a triangular structure.

Swadhishthana: The rivers of all the fluids of the universe are at this centre. Visualize the crescent moon and feel its coolness.

Manipura: Visualize here a fire, burning upwards, turning non-living matter into energy. Fill yourself with this pranic energy, this life force.

Anahata: Visualize upward and downward intersecting triangles filled with a pure white light. Feel this aura of purity, peace and brilliance.

Vishuddha: Visualize a pure blue sky, no stars, no blemishes, only silence and tranquility.

Ajna: Here shines a pure white flame which consumes all your karmas. Celestial sounds and lights may be experienced here.

2 exhalations and inhalations

Head and face:
Relax the eyebrow center, eyebrows, forehead, and top of
  the head. Breathe deeply with your entire body.

OM, shanti, shanti, shantihi.
OM, peace, peace, peace.

Chapter 6
Going Beyond

This chapter is titled, "Going Beyond," because it presents kriyas that can take one beyond body, breath and mind into the presence of the Inner One. The kriyas presented here comprise the last three limbs of Raja Yoga, namely dharana (concentration), dhyana (meditation) and samadhi (realization). Dharana is focusing the mind and making it one-pointed. For focusing the mind, one needs an object of concentration. In the kriyas of this chapter, the mind is focused on the breath, or on a chakra (energy center), or on specific visualizations.

Concentration, when sustained and prolonged, develops into meditation. Meditation should be steady and unbroken like the unbroken flow of a stream of oil. In meditation, one becomes aware of the gaps, the silence experienced between two thoughts. It seeks to expand the silence, so that there are no thoughts and no gaps. Meditation is described in Sanskrit as nirvishayam, that is without an object.

The kriyas like the 61 point exercise and shitali karana are preliminaries to the practice of yoga nidra. Yoga nidra, or yogic sleep has also been described as sleepless sleep or conscious sleep. The very simple but subtle OM kriya takes one to the fringes of samadhi and complements the practice of yoga nidra.

Manasa Pooja (Mental Worship)
There are three schools of *tantra: kaula, mishra* and *samaya.* Those who follow the kaula marga (path), try

to awaken kundalini shakti in the muladhara chakra at the base of the spine. This path involves physical rituals including sexual practices. This path has been misused by the ignorant. Mishra means mixed. In this path, there is inner worship mixed with external practices. Kundalini is awakened and worshipped at the heart center. The highest and purest form of tantra, is the samaya marga. It is purely yogic with absolutely no rituals. In this path, kundalini is awakened and worshipped in the thousand-petalled lotus at the crown of the head. The Saundaryalahiri (Wave of Beauty) of Adi Shankara is the principal scripture in samaya marga.

Yogis in subtle states of meditation realized that the center of spiritual consciousness is the lotus of the heart situated between the abdomen and thorax. They found that this lotus shines with a brilliant inner light. One of the yoga Upanishads states that supreme heaven shines in the lotus of the heart.

The Chandogya Upanishad has some beautiful passages describing the heart lotus. It states that in the city of Brahman (Brahmapuri), there is a mansion in the shape of a small lotus. The small inner space of this heart lotus is no different from the larger cosmic space. What is within this, should be sought and meditated upon. The Upanishad goes on to say that that which resides in the heart lotus, the Atman, does not age with the aging of the body nor does it perish with the death of the body. It is free from hunger, free from thirst and free from sorrow and free from evil. It desires only Truth and is resolved in Truth.

The method of meditation described here provides a locus for meditating upon supreme consciousness. Imagine that the body is a busy, bustling city, full of noises and distractions. In the heart of the city is a small shrine, and within this shrine dwells Atman. No matter how busy and noisy the streets of the city are, one can always retreat into the silence of this shrine and seek the "peace that passeth all understanding."

The Practice

First go through a systematic relaxation process in shavasana before beginning this kriya.

Do the following *sankalpa:* "The body is mine but I am not the body. The senses are mine but I am not the senses. The mind is mine but I am not the mind. My mind is only a witness. The ego is mine but I am not the ego. I am pure Atman. I am inhaling purity, exhaling all the subtle impressions from the subconscious mind. There is no sin for me. I am the virtuous one, a child of immortality and eternity. I will breathe in eternal life, exhaling all worries."

The ajna chakra is the gateway to the palace of the body. Enter the palace through this gateway and pass through the pure, illumined sky, free of clouds and stars, of the vishuddha chakra, to the anahata chakra.

At the anahata chakra, there are two intersecting, illumined triangles, one upward and the other downward, forming a star. In the center of the star is a temple of silence, totally free of all noise. Bathe in the courtyard of this temple and pluck five types of flowers: white, red, yellow, blue and pink. Enter the temple of silence.

In the temple, sit down facing the deity which is a circle of light, without a base, radiating blue and white light. Beside you are five golden utensils. Put the flowers into one of these utensils. The others contain water, *chandana* (sandalwood paste), incense and fruit.

Offer in turn the water, incense, chandana, flowers and fruits to the deity. There is light emanating from the center of the circle, illuminating the whole temple. There is perfect peace and silence.

Sit before the deity listening to your mantra emanating from the light. You do not say your mantra, you only listen to it. If you hear music, see lights or hear words, pay no attention. Only listen to your mantra. As you listen, you experience great bliss. You are a wave of bliss. Your body dissolves in an ocean of light. You are a ray of light of the cosmic sun. You are enjoying eternity, there is no birth or death. You are only aware of your mantra filling the temple of silence.

Now come out of the temple of silence, with folded hands, palms joined together, out of the intersecting upward and downward triangles of the heart center. Come up to the throat center and then to the eyebrow center.

Maintaining the peace you have experienced, rub your palms together and open your eyes to the darkness of your palms. Turn over to the left side and come into a sitting posture. You may now do your pranayama and *japa* or meditation.

Shitali Karana

This is a kriya that induces a very deep state of relaxation. It alleviates stress, reduces depression, reduces blood pressure and blood sugar and can help those who suffer from insomnia. The quality of sleep improves and the duration of sleep can be decreased. It is also a preliminary to the practice of yoga nidra (yogic sleep).

This exercise is performed in the corpse posture on the floor with a thin pillow supporting the neck and head. The room must be dark or a dark-colored blindfold used.

The sequence of steps is as follows:

Take five deep exhalations and inhalations, breathing diaphragmatically.

Now exhale from the crown of the head to the toes, emptying the whole body of fatigue, stress and toxins. Inhale from the toes, up through the ankles, knees, hip joints and spinal column to the crown. Feel that you are inhaling cosmic energy as you inhale. Repeat this for a total of 10 breaths.

Next exhale from the crown to the ankles, draining away all fatigue and stress. Inhale from the ankles to the crown, up through the knees, hip joints and spinal column to the crown, again feeling the inflow of cosmic energy. Repeat this 10 times.

Exhale from the crown to the knees and inhale from the knees to the crown. Repeat the process 10 times.

Now exhale from the crown to the perineum and inhale from the perineum to the crown, draining stress with exhalation and filling the body with energy with inhalation. Repeat the process five times (five breaths).

Similarly take five breaths from crown to the navel center and back, five breaths from the crown to the heart center and back, five breaths from the crown to the throat center and back.

Now exhale from the crown to the bridge between the nostrils and inhale from the nostrils to the crown for a total of five breaths with total awareness. Now the breath will be very fine and subtle.

Now exhale from the eyebrow center to the nostrils and inhale from the nostrils to the eyebrow center for a total of 10 breaths. You will notice that the pulse rate has decreased. The heart and involuntary nervous system will be rested.

Now the upward process is reversed and you start moving downwards. Exhale and inhale five times between the crown and the nostrils. Then exhale and inhale five times between the crown and the throat center, five times between the crown and heart center, five times between the crown and navel center and five times between the crown and perineum.

Continue with 10 breaths between the crown and the knees, 10 breaths between the crown and ankles and 10 breaths between the crown and the toes.

This completes the shitali karana kriya. Gently come out of shavasana.

Simple Yoga Nidra

In deep dreamless sleep, one is in the presence of the Self but without being consciously aware of the presence of the Self. A thin veil of Maya still separates one from the Self. Yoga nidra, on the other hand, is a state of conscious sleep. It is a half-sleep, half-waking state which confers a deeper state of rest than deep sleep. The body, smooth and striated muscles, nervous system and mind are all rested during yoga nidra. It releases stress, lowers the blood sugar and blood pressure, improves the circulation and can alleviate ulcers.

It is a state that can be used for learning things that are not as easily learnt while awake. There can be recording with an inner instrument during yoga nidra and complete recall of the recording when one comes out of yoga nidra. This was clearly demonstrated by H.H. Swami Rama in one of the experiments he performed at the Menninger Foundation in Topeka, Kansas, U.S.A. He went into a state of apparent sleep for about 20 minutes, producing predominantly the slow delta brain waves of deep sleep. When he came out of this state, he repeated more or less verbatim the conversation that took place in the laboratory during the 20 minutes.

The practice of yoga nidra is helpful in achieving control over the involuntary nervous system and also for developing one's intuition. However, there is still a fine demarcation between yoga nidra and the state of samadhi. The state of samadhi is the transitional state of consciousness between deep sleep and the transcendent state of turiya. Yoga nidra is a state of conscious sleep.

The simple variant of yoga nidra consists of a few breathing and mental exercises. To practice it, lie down on your back in the corpse posture (shavasana) in a quiet and undisturbed place, using a thin pillow and covering yourself with a blanket. The surface you lie on should be hard, and the pillow should be soft. Start doing diaphragmatic breathing. After 20 inhalations and exhalations, as you inhale, visualize an incoming wave of the ocean and as you exhale visualize the wave going back into the ocean. After 10 or 15 breaths, the shavayatra, 61 points exercise, should be carefully done.

Then learn to divest yourself of thoughts, feelings, and desires, but see that you do not touch the brink of sleep. The space between the two breasts, which is called anahata chakra, is the center where the mind rests during this practice. The mind should be focused on inhalation and exhalation only. While exhaling, the mind and breath are coordinated in a perfect manner. The mind observes that the inhalation and exhalation are functioning harmoniously. When the breath does not go through the stress of jerks and shallowness, and there is no unconscious expansion of the pause between inhalation and exhalation, then it establishes harmony. Beginners, for lack of practice, are trapped by inertia, and in most cases they experience going to the brink of sleep. This should be avoided in all cases. One should not pursue the practice at this state, but should just wake up and then repeat the same process the next day. This practice of emptying yourself and focusing on the breath should not be continued for more than 10 minutes in the beginning, and it should not be practiced more than once a day, for the mind has a habit of repeating its experience, both unconsciously and consciously. In habit formation, regularity, punctuality, and a systematic way of practice should be followed literally.

Advanced Yoga Nidra
Yoga nidra should be practiced either before sunrise or in the evening around sunset. It is best done after meditation.

One should not be sleepy or fatigued while doing yoga nidra. If possible, it should be done at the same time every day. Ideally the surroundings should be free of distracting noises and stimuli and the room should be made dark or a colored blindfold used. The practice actually starts after performing the preliminary practices of the 61 point exercise and shitali karana. What follows after these preliminaries should be done for only about 10 minutes in the beginning and one should use a gentle alarm to come out of the kriya.

In the advanced variant of yoga nidra, the following sequence is observed:

First do the 61 point exercise in shavasana.

This is then followed by the shitali kharana kriya.

Turn over from your back to the left side and breathe deeply from head to toe without going through individual points. This breathing helps with digestion by opening up the right or solar nostril. Feel as if the entire right side of the body is breathing. Do this for 10 breaths.

Then turn over to the right side and repeat the breathing process with 10 breaths, feeling as if the entire left side of the body is breathing.

Now shift to lying on your back and breathe with the whole body from head to toe. Feel the removal of stress, fatigue and toxins. Feel the incoming cosmic energy, energizing every pore of the body. Do this for 10 breaths.

Now bring your mind to the eyebrow center. Take three breaths at this center and let go of all distracting thoughts. Let go of your mantra too.

Shift your awareness with the breath to the throat center. Visualize a full moon shining at the throat center. This is very soothing. Stay at the throat center for several breaths.

Now come down with your awareness and breathing to the heart center between the two breasts. Continue to breathe diaphragmatically with smooth, serene breath, free of pauses. The breath will become very fine and subtle. Make sure that you do not come to the brink of sleep. Limit the practice of the actual kriya to about 10 minutes only in the beginning, till you achieve control of the feeling of sleep overcoming you. If you start feeling sleepy, come out of the kriya.

OM Kriya

Introduction

(Introduction with some minor editing from *OM, the Eternal Witness* by Swami Rama)

This kriya, or yogic practice, is a unique method for deepening your concentration and meditation. In this kriya, you can attain a state of deep bliss, like that of sleep, but you remain conscious. It is a state that is beyond sleep, between sleep and turiya. These exercises are not demonstrated or explained outside the monastery but can be practiced by those who have been doing sadhana, for many, many years. This kriya will help you. This method you can use for yourself and you can also use it on others; it is a scientific method. If you do not misuse it you can go ahead. It is very good for those who suffer from insomnia and cannot get a good night's rest. It also helps improve memory. Do this practice when you are not tired, when you are not going to sleep, when your tummy is not a pantry, when you are not very hungry, and when you have not eaten. You can do it at any time but it should not be done for sleep. This is a very good technique, a very therapeutic technique, but it should be done regularly. Habits, engagements, desires, break that which is called persistence. When a doctor says to use a medicine for 10 days, how does he know that in 10 days time you will be all right? It means that he has done experiments before with the drug. So is the case with this science. If you persist for some time, I can tell you, after so many days, this is going to happen, after so many days, that is going to happen. But if you do not practice, but just want to know, that is not right knowledge. Practice and help yourself. Perhaps you'll find a new vision, perhaps you'll find something new.

This kriya is done in a posture that is called shavasana. Shavasana means corpse pose. You lie down on your back in this posture, called shavasana, with your heels spread apart and with your arms away from the body, palms upward and fingers gently curled. Corpse pose means you should entirely pose like a corpse. Corpse does not speak, does not see, hear, or move; if somebody hits the corpse, it does not open its eyes. First, you should learn to acquire that state which is called the corpse pose, though your consciousness will be there. You should be fully conscious, but put your body in that position. One of the highest poses is the corpse pose; in itself, it is perfect.

The word shava, means corpse. What is this word? Why is it called shava? It is missing something, it is missing shakti. Shiva, without shakti, becomes shava. If you don't have energy, you are inert, mere shava, mere corpse. During that time you should not be active at all. Make your body completely inactive but comfortable and conscious. Then you are relaxing. How will you relax? Not with suggestions, no. Suggestions will give poor relaxation, a hypnotic relaxation. If, instead, you exhale and allow your mind to flow with breath, then all toxins will be expelled because you are lengthening the exhalation. All the carbon dioxide, used up gas, will rush to the lungs, the storehouse, and be expelled.

There are very few people for whom this posture is not suitable; most people like to lie down. There are, however, two obstacles in this posture. First, you might go to sleep and second, you might urinate; it can happen if your bladder has lost its power of conduction. That is why Shankaracharya and other yogis, did not recommend this. But if you decide you are not going to sleep, no matter in which posture you practice, you can deepen your meditation in this posture definitely. It's as definite as 2 plus 2 equals 4, not 5. Whether you are good or bad, whether you are a sage or a criminal, this will definitely deepen your concentration.

The room should not be very warm, nor very cold. The floor should not be very hard, nor should it be very uneven. Do not do this practice on a waterbed! The floor may be hard, but you can put a mattress on it and use a soft pillow. The pillow should be soft and the bed should be hard, remember this. Always use a pillow, thin pillow, otherwise, sometimes *urdva vayu* or apana vayu, the gastric gases, may create a disturbance. Upward movement of the apana, used up gas, should not disturb you. If you complain of an aching body, first look at what type of bed you use. What type of pillow do you use? If you twist the pillow and insert it under the neck, in the morning you will feel some pain and the doctors will advise you to wear a collar. Many a time you change from side to side and use a hard pillow and that disturbs you. Often the bed disturbs you. Make your room less bright, without harsh lights that distract your eyes.

Lie down in shavasana. Gently close your eyes and physically relax your limbs, all limbs, systematically upwards from toes to your head and again come down, just physically relaxing. Start breathing diaphragmatically; this is very helpful. Then, as I told you, let your mind follow the breath. The easiest and best way of concentrating the mind is to let the mind flow with the breath. The mind is very close to breath, but the mind is not sincere to the breath. A husband may not be sincere with his wife, running here and there. The mind is like that man, while the breath is like a mother, they have different natures. A mother tries to control the father in her own way; so if you approach through your mother you can easily have access to your father. But if you approach your father first, perhaps you will meet with denial. Through breath, you should learn to approach your mind, for mind and breath are twin laws of life. For a few minutes do diaphragmatic breathing, this is very helpful. That should become a habit.

Try to relax your limbs and muscles as much as you can. First you have to exhale, that's called rechaka. Let your mind flow with your breath, because they are the greatest of friends in the world. No one can attain as good a friendship as mind and breath. If mind wants to distract breath, breath is always distracted; you will not be healthy. If breath is calm, it can always help to make your mind calm. Now you are allowing your mind to flow with the breath, exhaling. When you go beyond your capacity in exhalation, there will be a jerk. You have to watch your capacity. So you should work with the digital system. First you should use a ratio of 8 to 4, exhalation to a count of 8 and inhalation to a count of 4. This is the starting ratio. Later, it can be increased. Any respiratory problem or any emotional problem can be nipped by this method; it's very therapeutic, for mind and for the breath. It's very good for the heart, nervous system, and brain. Your memory will improve if you follow this method. We are bypassing many breathing exercises, nadi shodhanam or channel purification, other exercises like *antar* (internal) and *bahya* (external) *kumbhaka* (retention), *plavni*, etc. We are bypassing all this in establishing this kriya.

The first exhalation is from the bridge between the nostrils to the top of the crown and then down, to the space between your heels. Then you are inhaling from the space between the heels to the top of the crown. After that, you are inhaling and exhaling from the top of the crown (see Figure 26). If you have not practiced to lengthen your breath, then exhale only up to the point, where both legs unite, called muladhara chakra. There is a triangular cavity at the base of the spinal column where kundalini shakti sleeps, called power of powers, coiled, some say 2-1/2 feet, but definitely 2-1/2 times. It is here in this cavity. Many names are given to it. When she is sleeping here, we are in the waking state. Because she is sleeping here, we are still brutes. Why is she sleeping here? Because she's intoxicated; the power of consciousness is the intoxicant. What happened? When you are intoxicated you forget your home, your own home. Her real home is actually at swadhisthana chakra, the pelvic center. But because of intoxication, she forgets and she is sleeping at muladhara. Swadhisthana is her own abode. *Swa* means own, *adhisthana* means abode. Yogis learn to awaken that sleeping serpent energy.

If you can, try to go with the length of the breath; that will be very useful to you. Yogis even measure how many inches the breath flows during exhalation, 4 inches, 8 inches, 10 inches. As you are exhaling, let your mind follow. Don't create a pause, start inhaling, going to the crown of your head. Again with no pause, start exhaling from the top of the crown to the space between the two feet again. Only the first exhalation is from the space between the nostrils. After that, you exhale from the top of the crown. Initially, you should do five exhalations and inhalations. Then, gradually increase the number to 100 exhalations and inhalations.

If you have not practiced lengthening exhalation, better exhale up to the muladhara chakra first, after a month or two you can go up to the space between your feet. After three to four months you can make a point somewhere in the distance, feel as though you are exhaling to that distance, to that point, and inhaling from there. Do not visualize a wall in front of you; let there be a clear blue sky. You can gradually increase the distance mentally. Now there are two aspects. One is called *door darshita*, seeing far and wide.

You can see something beyond the walls. The other is called *sukshma darshita,* seeing the subtlest. You can see the subtlest thing. A small pin is dropped here; immediately you come and see it.

Now, slowly as you learn to expand the length of exhalation, go on expanding, don't visualize any wall in front of you, visualize an open window, visualize as though you are going towards the horizon, towards space. Where does this stream of exhalation go? You'll find that it flows into a pool, the stream becomes one with the pool. This is a pool of cosmic energy. Now you are going to inhale. Here's something very mysterious. From where are you inhaling? You are not inhaling from the nostrils. From where are you inhaling? You are inhaling from the pool of cosmic energy, filling yourself to the depths of your being. Who is giving you this life breath? We take different foods, we have different thoughts, but we have only one air to inhale. There is only one proprietor who is giving us air to inhale. That means there is only one proprietor of your body. The Mandukya Upanishad says it is *prajna,* asleep in the city of life. How can you go to the city of life? When you go there you should not fall asleep. If you know the technique of being awake, yet, being there, then you will know that *Purusha.* You can enjoy His presence with yoga nidra; it can be done.

When you exhale, you have a feeling of emptying yourself. In inhalation you reverse that feeling by filling up your whole being which you have emptied. One feeling you use when you exhale, another feeling you use when you inhale. Otherwise, you may remain in that state and lose touch with the life force and remain inactive. With one feeling you empty your whole system, with a different feeling you fill up that system. What mantra can you use? You can use OM, it's very supportive. Mantra is a great support. When do you need support? When you are weak, mantra is a great support. You should have friendship with the mantra, then it helps you whenever you need. You are remembering the mantra OM, a single syllable. Your feeling will be entirely different when you do this kriya. No matter how much meditation you have done, you will be transported into a different realm when you start doing this kriya.

Now when you are doing this you can use OM, because OM will direct the flow. It's like that fish that does not touch either shore, but only follows the flow. It is like that bird who flies freely in the blue sky. So you are exhaling, not mere exhaling, but with OM. Half of the sound is *OOOO* and half is *MMMM*, OM. And then you are in state of *amatra*, you have gone to silence. Mind should watch the breath with only one OM during inhalation, another OM during exhalation. As a sound, it's only one sound.

There are three channels in your body. The channel in the center is called centralis canalis and on both sides are two ganglionated cords. Energy is flowing through the central channel, and kundalini is residing at the base. "A" originates from the top of the crown, "U" rolls and by the time you reach the end of exhalation, it becomes "M," then silence. Then, you come back the same way to the top of the crown. You see that breath passes through that channel called centralis canalis, the middle channel. You can go beyond the body, it will go, let it go, but as long as you are in the body, there is a system.

During exhalation, feel that you are emptying your body. You can easily locate the tension points in your body. Now when inhaling, feel that you are filling up to the depths of your being, the energy received from the atmosphere, from the cosmos. That's a true feeling, that's not something artificial. While exhaling, see how far you can go with your breath stream. After visualizing that distant point, come back filling to the depths of your being, with fresh energy.

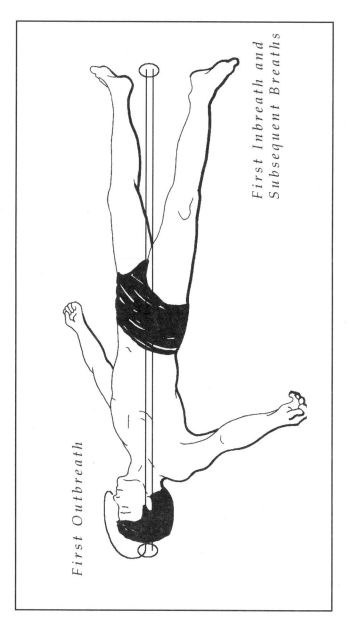

Figure 26

You should not visualize a wall in front of you. You should visualize a clear, blue sky. Every time you exhale, you have to advance a little further with the stream of your breath. Let me see how far you can go with the stream of breath when you are exhaling. And your mind should flow with the breath, it should not run here and there, leaving that stream of breath. Then pull in the stream of energy from that distant point, filling your whole depth. Because you are doing this with breath awareness, it is not self-hypnosis. If you are not doing it with breath awareness, then you are only giving suggestions to yourself. "You should go to sleep, you should go to sleep, you should go to sleep." This is called self-suggestion. Now, for some time let your mind flow with the breath. If anything intervenes, you understand what is intervening, something very important, something very ugly, bad habit of yours, or something important which you have forgotten to do.

Your breath should not be jerky; it should not be noisy; it should be calm. Let your mind flow with the flow of the breath, but during that flow, when you are exhaling, you are exhaling all that you have; you want to throw away everything that you have. If a glass is full, how will you put something in it? You will have to empty it first. Even the empty glass has something in it called air. When you fill it, then it will be filled. That is the process. Some people, no matter how old they are, look very fresh, young, because of this practice. Your skin will change, that's the first symptom. Your skin will become very smooth like silk; your face will become very loving, your eyes will become very piercing. These are certain symptoms I observe in students.

You might not feel like coming back. Slowly you'll find your body is really floating, it might even float in space, and it's not difficult. But you will find slowly that floating experience will give you great joy. You should practice systematically, step by step. Don't jump. Learn to be patient with yourself. Always have an alarm clock for this practice, so that you will not be afraid, but will come out at the right time. You should use an alarm clock or ask somebody to wake you up at the right time. Now, you have to follow the system.

Choose a time for this kriya when all interruptions are avoided. After 10 days, 15 days, one month you can expand your exhalation beyond the muladhara chakra to the space between your feet. If you do it for 15-20 days, you will feel elevated; you will find your personality has changed; your thinking has changed; and your memory has sharpened. This is not a mere statement; this is a fact. What problem will you find? All the bad things arising from shallow breath, all the diseases connected with shallow breath, diseases coming from jerky breath, diseases coming from noisy breath, diseases coming from pause. It's a very therapeutic practice. If you are a therapist, you can teach your patients this practice, and even monitor their progress, without seeing them, from a distance.

You will have many, many, many wonderful experiences. Don't push yourself, go according to your capacity otherwise you will feel as though someone is squeezing you. Increase your capacity gradually. Initially you were going further and further with exhalation. To complete the kriya, you have to reverse this. Slowly you will have to learn to come back, come back gradually with the same ratio. Voluntarily you reverse the expansion and bring it back to this point between the two nostrils. During that time, your inhalation and exhalation are very fine and you are exhaling and inhaling between the eyebrow center and the bridge between the nostrils. The brain has a reserve of prana for about three minutes, after which the brain starts degenerating. As you can live for two to three days without eating food because of body reserves, so also with prana, there is a reserve for about three minutes. After two and a half to three minutes the brain starts degenerating and that's called death. You are conscious, but you float in great joy, you might even levitate, provided you have done it perfectly. It may take three to six months to attain this, but joy you will attain the very first day you start practicing.

So when you are exhaling and allowing your mind to flow, the whole body is getting relaxed. I once demonstrated that when the body is completely relaxed, you cannot lift that body easily. It will take six or seven people to lift the same body, which is normally lifted by two people. Heaviness is a symptom of how relaxed the body is. But it's only at the level of body consciousness. You should feel delight in relaxation, but you should not become afraid. In the beginning, do not practice more than five minutes. Do you know that 10 minutes practice with one-pointed mind will lead you to samadhi? Some of you say that you meditate for two hours. I say no. You sit for two hours of course, but you do not meditate for two hours. Your effort is to make your mind flow towards its target, aim without any interruption. You can do it with the help of this kriya.

There are four main states of consciousness, waking, dream, deep sleep and turiya. Then there are three intermediate or transitional states, unmani, ahladini and samadhi, making a total of seven states. (See Figure 3, Chapter 1). Between waking and dreaming, is the intermediate state called unmani. Between dreaming and sleeping is the intermediate state called ahladini. Between sleep and turiya, is the intermediate state called samadhi. If you perfect this kriya, then it will become easy for you to do yoga nidra. Yoga nidra is very close to samadhi. Yoga nidra is also called sleepless sleep or voluntary sleep. In sleepless sleep you are in deep samadhi, yet you are fully conscious. Many of you think that in deep samadhi, you are not aware. No, no, no, your awareness expands. Don't lose your awareness in any situation. When your awareness slips to the valley of absent-mindedness, that's not a good sign. It should be intact.

For a few days interruptions will come. When these interruptions start decreasing, you'll find that the mind is flowing freely with the breath, breath is flowing freely with the mind, and there is great joy. During that time, sushumna is activated. Sushumna means sukha mana, peaceful mind, joyous mind, serene breath and calm mind. That state which is given by serene breath and calm mind is called sushumna, where both nostrils start flowing freely. Neither nostril is predominant, both start flowing freely. And when they both flow freely, you cannot cry, you cannot have pain, you cannot have sadness, because that state of breath leads your mind to a state of joyous mind.

Now, medical science says that you have more than 10 billion brain cells, but those cells are constantly dying, and there is no rejuvenation of the brain cells according to medical science. But a yogi says, of course, they can be rejuvenated. We never say that all the dead cells can come back to life, like with Christ. We don't say that, but we have a method of not allowing the cells to die. How will it help you? If out of 10 billion cells, a few cells die every day, who cares? Well, in old age you lose your memory, you lose your physical coordination, you may even become insane. The brain is the seat of the mind which is energy; the brain is a physical part. If you constantly blast my seat, I will be disturbed all the time. Don't constantly blast your brain. You are blasting your brain because you are not breathing well. You are blasting your brain through bad food. You are blasting your brain with negative feedback: you are good for nothing, you are bad, you are this, you are that; as you talk to your husband you are talking to yourself. If you are saying something to somebody, it means you are talking to yourself, you are saying the same thing to yourself. It's a projection of your mind. So don't do that, stop blasting.

How? Mind will do it, so you have to keep your mind busy all the time so mind doesn't do that. Whenever the mind is idle, give it some work. Don't allow the mind to be free, it can become the workshop of the devil. That is why you have to remember the center of consciousness within. Those who are Jewish, can remember some sort of confirmation which they use, prayer, compact prayer. Those who are Christian can use some saying of Christ. Those who are Hindu can use some mantra. Otherwise you can use the method recommended by the Upanishad that your state is the fourth, turiya. You are a citizen of the fourth, and the three countries for which you have a visa to travel freely are waking, dreaming and sleeping. But where is your real country? Your real country is turiya, it is your permanent abode. With this type of thinking, you can slowly reduce wandering from this country to that country and stay in your own native place that is called turiya, the state beyond waking, dreaming, and sleeping.

Summary of the OM Kriya Technique

Lie on the floor in shavasana with a thin pillow under the head and a dark handkerchief covering the eyes.

This kriya is done with 2:1 breathing, that is exhalation being twice as long as the inhalation, the mental chanting of the mantra Ooooommmmm being coordinated with the length of the breath.

To establish the 2:1 breathing rhythm, one can use a mental count but this creates slight jerks in the breath. Another method is to exhale from the crown, along the spinal column to the space midway between the heels and to inhale from the muladhara chakra to the crown. The kriya begins once you have established the rhythm of 2:1 breathing.

The first exhalation of the kriya is from the space between the nostrils to the ajna chakra, then to the crown and going down to the back of the head and down along sushumna to the muladhara chakra and then to the point midway between the heels, chanting Ooooommmmm mentally with the exhalation. You inhale from the point beween the heels to the muladhara chakra and then to the crown along sushumna, chanting Ooooommmmm mentally with inhalation. The mind should flow with breath using the OM chant for focusing the mind. You exhale into the cosmic pool of prana and inhale from this cosmic pool.

After the first exhalation, all other exhalations are from the crown to the space between the heels and inhalations from the space between the heels to the crown. If your breathing capacity is limited, you can initially exhale and inhale between the crown and muladhara rather than to the point between the heels.

Practice this kriya initially only for 5-10 minutes, staying within your capacity. You can use a soft alarm to get you out of the kriya.

As you progress, you can expand your exhalation, starting from the crown to the muladhara, then from the crown to the space between the heels, continuing to a point further away and finally to the horizon, visualizing a clear blue sky, not a wall in front of you. Maintain the 2:1 rhythm and stay within your capacity.

After you have learnt to expand your exhalation to the horizon, you have to then learn the reverse process of contraction but making the breath very subtle. You will finally be breathing between the ajna chakra and the space between the nostrils with very subtle breath.

The body will initially feel very heavy due to deep relaxation but will gradually feel very light as this practice deepens. This kriya will make it easier for you to practice yoga nidra which will then lead you very close to samadhi, a state between deep sleep and turiya.

Bhuta Shuddhi
(Purification of the Bhutas or Elements of the Body)

This kriya is done before meditation. It has been given to us by the great Adi Shankara. It is from the samaya marga tradition and can not only purify the *bhutas* but also the *samskaras* which are the latent seed tendencies derived from past experiences and stored in the unconscious mind.

Lie down on the floor, preferably a wooden floor, on your back, with knees bent and drawn up, feet on the floor and palms downward on the floor. The back should be flat against the floor without a gap. Use a thin pillow for the head. Cover your eyes with a dark colored handkerchief.

Exhale from the crown to your toes, releasing all tensions, stains, wrong actions, karmas. Inhale *atma tattwa* from your toes to the crown, to the depth of your being. Exhale and inhale 10 times between the crown and toes.

Now exhale from the crown to the toes and inhale from the ankles to the crown. Repeat five times.

Next exhale from the crown to the ankles and inhale from the knees to the crown. Repeat five times.

Then exhale from the crown to the knees and inhale from the muladhara chakra to the crown. Repeat five times.

Continue this process with exhalation to the muladhara, swadhishthana, manipura, anahata and vishuddha chakras and inhalation from the chakra just above it, repeating the process five times.

Exhale from the crown to the vishuddha chakra and inhale from the ajna (pit at back of head) to the crown. The breath becomes very fine and subtle. Exhale to the ajna chakra and inhale at the crown five times.

Do this practice for 41 days without a break, three times a day if possible. Then you are prepared to tread the path of samaya. Observe brahmacharya during the 41-day practice.

Basic Meditation

Sit in a stable, comfortable posture with the head, neck and trunk aligned and erect. Gently close your eyes. Mentally survey the body from the crown of the head downwards. Release tension in the forehead, cheeks, mouth and jaws. Release tension in the neck and shoulders. Release all tension in the arms, palms and fingers. Come back up with the mind to the shoulders and chest. Take several deep breaths making sure that the breathing is diaphragmatic, deep, smooth, quiet and free of pauses. Surrender all tension and fill yourself with peace and serenity. Move down with the mind, releasing tension from the navel, lower abdomen, pelvis, hips, thighs, knees, calves, ankles and feet. Exhale and inhale deeply five to 10 times, exhaling through the toes and inhaling from the toes all the way to the crown. Visualizing the various parts of the body, move upwards with the mind, relaxing the various parts of the body. If there is tension, discomfort or pain in any part of the body, go mentally to that part and consciously relax that part.

So-Ham Meditation

This is a second exercise of meditation. Sit in a stable, comfortable posture with the head, neck and trunk aligned and erect. Gently close your eyes. After mentally surveying the body from head to toe and back and releasing any tension, start paying attention to your breathing. Exhale as though you are exhaling from the crown of the head to the base of the spine with the breath flowing through the innermost channel of the spinal cord, the canalis centralis. Mentally chant *Hummmm* . . . with the exhalation till you reach the base of the spine. Without a pause, start inhaling from the base of the spine to the crown of the head, through the canalis centralis, mentally chanting *Sooo* . . . till you reach the crown. Continue exhaling and inhaling through the spine with full awareness of the breath, the mental chanting of so-ham and the passage of the breath through the spine. Let the breath and mind flow together. Feel the subtle energy current flowing between the medulla oblongata (base of the brain) and the pelvic plexus in a continuous loop. If the mind gets distracted, it will be sensed as a jerk or irregularity in the breath. Bring the wandering mind back to breath awareness, the spinal pathway and the so-ham mantra. If one of the nostrils is blocked, fix your awareness on the blocked nostril till it opens up. Let the breath flow through both nostrils making the mind joyous. In the beginning, do not sit for more than 10–15 minutes in meditation. If your mind becomes restless and turbulent, come out of meditation. When you come out of meditation, rub your palms together creating some warmth and gently open your eyes to the darkness of your warm palms.

Guru Chakra and Ajna Chakra Meditation

After nadi shodhanam, concentrate on the open nostril for one minute.

Then switch your awareness to the passive nostril till it opens up.

Now go back to the first nostril, and just as it opens, go into sushumna, breathing in from the space between the two nostrils to the ajna chakra and back. Let the breath flow equally through both nostrils.

Now stay at ajna chakra for a few breaths and then go up to guru chakra.

At *guru chakra* you perform the *havan* (fire sacrifice) to the blazing fire. You offer up your distracting thoughts, bad habits, desires, etc. With each offering you mentally say, *guruve svaha, na mama* (unto the Guru, not mine). At the end of the havan, you chant mentally *guruve namaha* three times.

Now come down to ajna chakra and enter into a dark tunnel that is between the eyebrow center and the back of the skull called *brahmar guha* (cave of the bee). As you mentally repeat your mantra, listen to its echo from the walls of this tunnel. As the echo becomes more distinct, just listen to the mantra without consciously repeating it.

Now imagine a taut string between the back of the skull and the base of the spine. Move down with your outbreath to the base of the spine and up with the inbreath to the back of the skull. Let the mind and breath flow together.

Come back to ajna chakra for a few breaths.

Then breathe between the ajna chakra and the space between the nostrils.

Now limit your awareness to the breath in the nostrils, warm outbreath and cool inbreath. Rub your palms together and slowly open your eyes into the hollow of your palms.

Asato ma sada gamaya
Lead me from untruth (unreal) to the truth,
Tamaso ma jyotir gamaya
Lead me from darkness to light,
Mrityor ma amritam gamaya
Lead me from mortality to immortality.

OM saha navavatu
OM may Braham protect us together,
Saha nau bhunaktu
May He nourish us together,
Saha viryam karavavahai
May we gather strength working together,
Tejasvi navadhitam astu
May our study illumine us and become purposeful,

Ma vidvishavahai
May unity and love prevail between us,
OM Shanti Shanti Shantihi
OM Peace Peace Peace.

Annexure 1
Suggested Practice Plan

The Himalayan Tradition emphasizes the integration of body, breath and mind. So the Suggested Practice Plan includes all three dimensions at beginner, intermediate and advanced stages of practice. The duration of time in each stage before moving to the next stage is dependent on the time available for practice and the motivation of the practitioner. In each dimension, the practices suggested at a particular stage can be added on to the practices of the earlier stage, again time permitting. In the advanced stage, the practitioner can use his/her discrimination to create a routine that fits in with time and schedule constraints.

The sequence usually followed is asanas, followed by relaxation, then pranayama and ending with a meditative technique. Asanas, other than child and boat asanas have not been dealt with in this manual. The sadhaka is advised to take the guidance of a yoga instructor in selecting asanas at the intermediate and advanced levels based on physical and medical condition.

Details of practices for body, breath and mind: Beginner, Intermediate and Advanced Stages

Stage	Body	Breath	Mind
Beginner	Joints and Glands Exercises	Diaphragmatic Breathing (Makarasana and Shavasana)	Relaxation of Muscles and Joints
	Cultivate a sitting posture with head neck and trunk aligned	Jala Neti (Nasal Wash with Water)	Beginning Tense-Relax Exercise
		Nadi Shodhanam (Alt. Nostril Breathing) Variation 1	31 Point Exercise
		Kapalabhati	Basic Meditation
		Bhastrika Variation 1	
Intermediate	Simpler Asanas including Child and Boat Asanas	Sandbag Breathing	Relaxation of Muscles, Joints and Chakras
	Ashwini Mudra	2:1 Breathing	Abbv. Relaxation of Muscles, Joints and Chakras

		Sutra Neti (Neti with String)	Intermediate Tense-Relax Exercise
		Nadi Shodhanam Variations 1, 2 & 3	61 Point Exercise
		Bhastrika Variations 1, 2 & 3	Soham Meditation
			Simple Yoga Nidra
Advanced	More Advanced Asanas	Add on Ujjayi	Advanced Tense-Relax Exercise
	Agni Sara	Add on Brahmari	77 Point Exercise
			Manasa Pooja (Mental Worship)
			Shitali Karana
			Advanced Yoga Nidra
			OM Kriya
			Bhuta Shuddhi
			Guru Chakra and Ajna Chakra Meditation

Suggested Learning Sequences

Chapter 2: Stilling the Body

Beginning Level
Shavasana (corpse pose)
Makarasana (crocodile pose)
Boat pose
Child's pose
Maitreyi asana (friendship pose)
Sukhasana (easy pose)
Swastikasana (auspicious pose)
Siddhasana (accomplished pose)

Intermediate Level
Ashwini mudra (buttock roll)
Padmasana (lotus pose)
Agnisara

Chapter 4: Stilling the Breath

Beginning Level
Diaphragmatic breathing
Jala neti (nasal wash with water)
Nadi shodhanam (alternate nostril breathing), variation 1
Sushumna application
Kapalabhati
Bhastrika variation 1

Intermediate Level
Sandbag breathing
2:1 breathing
Sutra neti (neti with string)

Nadi shodhanam variations 1, 2 & 3
Bhastrika variations 1, 2 & 3
Ujjayi
Brahmari

Chapter 5: Stilling the Senses and Mind through Relaxation

Beginning Level
Relaxation of muscles and joints
Beginning tense-relax exercise
31 point exercise

Intermediate Level
Intermediate tense-relax exercise
61 point exercise
Relaxation of muscles, joints and chakras
Abbv. relaxation of muscles, joints and chakras

Advanced Level
Advanced tense-relax exercise
77 point exercise

Chapter 6: Going Beyond

Beginning Level
Basic meditation
Soham meditation

Intermediate Level
Simple Yoga Nidra

Advanced Level
Manasa pooja (mental worship)
Shitali kharana
Advanced yoga nidra
OM kriya
Bhuta shuddhi
Guru chakra and ajna chakra meditation

Suggested Reading List of Books of the Himalayan Tradition

The list below is arranged in a progressive sequence of sadhana development and advancement.

A Practical Guide to Holistic Health
Holistic Living Manual
Science of Breath
Meditation and its Practice
Conscious Living and/or *Art of Joyful Living*
Path of Fire and Light Vol. 2
Path of Fire and Light Vol. 1 (more advanced practices)
OM: The Eternal Witness
Perennial Psychology of the Bhagavad Gita

A 2-volume audio CD set (Practices of the Himalayan Tradition as Taught by Swami Rama) is also available for guided practices. Volume 1 covers many of the basic level practices and Volume 2 includes some intermediate and advanced level practices.

Glossary

ADHISTHANA   Original state

ADI PRANA   Primal or original vital principle (prana), the first unit of life connecting the mind with the Atma or center of consciousness

AGNISARA   A yogic kriya for strengthenig the abdominal muscles and navel center

AHLADINI   A transitional state of consciousness between the dreaming and deep sleep states

AJNA CHAKRA   The eyebrow center, the seat of the mind

AKASHA   The space element

AMATRA   Without measure, boundless

ANAHATA CHAKRA   The heart center, seat of the air element

ANTAR   Inner

APANA VAYU   One of the five major vayus or vital forces associated with exhalation and excretion

APARNA   A name of the Divine Mother associated with her penitence of surviving only on air

ARTHA   One of the four aims of life, that of material prosperity

ASANA   Yogic posture

ASHRAMAS   Life stages

ASHTANGA   **Eight-limbed**

ASHWA   Sanskrit for horse

ASHWINI MUDRA   Contraction and relaxation of the anal muscles

ATMA TATTWA   Consciousness principle

BAHYA   Outer

BASTI   Yogic enema for cleansing the colon

BHASTRIKA   A pranayama technique involving forceful exhalation and inhalation

BHATI   Shines

BHUTA SHUDDHI   Yogic technique for purifying the five bhutas or elements comprising the physical body

BHUTAS   The five elements of the universe (macrocosm) and body (microcosm), namely earth, water, fire, air and space

BRAHMACHARYA   Literally walking in Brahman, the Supreme One; often connotes control of the sensual urges

BRAHMAN   The Supreme One

BRAHMAPURI   The city of Brahman

BRAHMAR GUHA   Cave of the bee

BRAHMARI   A pranayama technique creating the sound of a humming bee

CHAKRA   Literally wheel, center of energy and consciousness along the spinal column

CHANDANA   Sandalwood paste

DHARANA   Concentration

DHARMA   Ethical codes that support a harmonious society

DHAUTI   Yogic cleansing technique requiring the swallowing of a long piece of cloth

DHYANA   Meditation

DOOR DARSHITA   Far seeing

GRIHASTA   Householder

GURU CHAKRA   Center of consciousness above the eyebrow center

GURUVE NAMAHA   Bow to the Guru

GURUVE SVAHA, NA MAMA   Offered unto the Guru, not mine

HATHA YOGA   Physical or outer yoga comprising the lower four rungs of the eight-limbed Raja Yoga with emphasis on asanas and pranayama

HAVAN   Fire ritual

IDA   Channel of prana that originates at the base of the spine and terminates in the left nostril

JALA NETI   Yogic technique for cleansing the nasal passages with salt water

JALANDHARA BANDHA   Chin lock

JAPA   Mantra repetition usually using a mala (rosary)

JIVAS   Individual souls

JNANENDRIYAS   Cognitive senses

KAMA   Desire, passion

KAPALA   Skull

KAPALABHATI   Pranayama technique with forceful exhalation and passive inhalation that is said to make the skull shine

KARMENDRIYAS   Active senses

KAULA   A path of tantra

KHANDA   Root between anus and genitals, the body's solar system

KRIYA   Yogic practice derived from the root 'kri,' meaning to act

KUMBHAKA   Breath retention

KUNDALINI SHAKTI   Coiled up sleeping (potential) energy at base of spinal column

MAITREYI ASANA   Friendship pose, sitting on a chair with hands resting on knees

MAKARASANA   Crocodile posture used to learn diaphragmatic breathing

MANASA POOJA   Mental worship

MANIPURA CHAKRA   Navel center

MARGA   Path

MAYA   Power of illusion that makes the unreal seem real and the transient seem permanent

MISHRA Mixed

MOKSHA Self-realization, spiritual emancipation, nirvana

MULADHARA BANDHA Root lock

NADI SHODHANAM Pranayama technique for cleansing the pranic channels called nadis, alternate nostril breathing

NAULI Yogic cleansing technique involving rolling of the abominal muscles from side to side

NIRVISHAYAM Without an object

NIYAMAS Second limb of the eight-limbed Raja Yoga comprising the five observances of purity, contentment, spiritual disciplines, scriptural study and surrender

OM KRIYA A special yogic technique utilizing the mental chanting of OM with 2 :1 breathing

PADMASANA Lotus posture

PANCHA SNANA Washing five limbs: two hands, face, and two feet

PINGALA Channel of prana that originates at the base of the spine and terminates in the right nostril

PLAVNI Yogic technique of breath retention that results in loss of consciousness

PRAJNA State of consciousness associated with deep, dreamless sleep

PRANA Vital force or energy

PRANAYAMA Yogic technique for regulation and expansion of prana

PRATYAHARA Withdrawal of the senses

PURUSHA Male principle in Sankhya Yoga, denoting the consciousness principle

PURUSHARTHAS The four main aims of human existence, namely dharma, artha, kama and moksha

RAJA YOGA Eight-limbed path of yoga

RECHAKA Exhalation

SADHAKA   Spiritual aspirant

SAMADHI   Transitional state of consciousness between deep sleep and turiya, also the last rung of Raja Yoga

SAMAYA   The highest tantric path

SAMSKARAS   Latent seed tendencies, derived from past experiences and buried in the unconscious mind

SANDHYA   Joining, usually used for sunrise or sunset where the solar and lunar energies are joined

SANKALPA   Determination, resolve

SANNYASA   Renunciation

SHAT KRIYAS   Six cleansing techniques, namely neti, dhauti, nauli, basti, kapalabhati and trataka

SHAVA   Corpse

SHAVASANA   Corpse Pose

SHAVYATRA   Literally, pilgrimage around the corpse, yogic technique of journeying with awareness through specific energy points of the body

SHITALI KARANA   Yogic technique utilizing breath awareness

SIDDHASANA   Accomplished pose

SO-HAM   Generic mantra of breath awareness, where the sound *sooo* is mentally chanted during inhalation and *hummm* during exhalation

STHIRA   Stable

SUKHA   Comfortable

SUKHA MANAH   Joyous mind

SUKHASANA   Easy pose

SUKSHMA DARSHITA   Subtle sight

SUSHUMNA   Central channel of pranic flow along spinal column

SUSHUMNA APPLICATION   Breath awareness technique to facilitate opening of both nostrils to open and energize sushumna

SUTRA NETI   Cleansing of the nasal passages with a waxed string or rubber catheter

SWA   Oneself

SWADHISTHANA CHAKRA   Pelvic energy center

SWADHYAYA   Self-study involving scriptural study, introspection and contemplation

SWASTIKASANA   Sitting posture where the folded legs resemble the swastika symbol

TANTRA   Branch of yoga utilizing mantra and yantra

TAPAS   Spirutual disciplines

TATTWAS   Subtle elements from which the five bhutas or gross elements are formed

TRATAKA   One of six cleansing techniques with concentrated gazing for making the mind one-pointed

TURIYA   The fourth state of consciousness beyond waking, dream and deep sleep

UDDIYANA BANDHA   Navel lock performed by lifting abdominal muscles

UJJAYI   Pranayama technique using partially clossed glottis

UNMANI   Transitional state of consciousness between waking and dreaming states

URDVA VAYU   Upward moving apana vayu, gastric gas

VANAPRASTHA   Forerst dweller, the third stage of life

VAYU   Air principle, that which flows

VISHUDDHA CHAKRA   Throat center

YAMAS   First limb of Raja Yoga of five constraints, namely non-hurting, non-lying, non-indulging of senses, non-stealing and non-attachment

YOGA   Yoke, union of individual soul (atma) and the Supreme (paramatma)

YOGA NIDRA   Yogic conscious sleep, sleepless sleep

About the Author

Dr. Prakash Keshaviah met H.H. Swami Rama in 1969 and was initiated into the Himalayan Tradition in 1971. A few years later, he was trained by Swami Rama to be a mantra initiator in the tradition.

Dr. Prakash is a Biomedical Scientist with a B.Tech. in Mechanical Engineering (I.I.T. Madras) and post-graduate degrees in Mech. Engg., Physiology and Biomedical Engineering from the University of Minnesota, U.S.A. He gained international recognition in the field of Dialysis through his scientific papers and patents.

After a 30-year career in the U.S., at the behest of Swami Rama, Prakash returned to India in 1998 to volunteer his services at the Himalayan Institute Hospital Trust. He established and manages the Dialysis Unit at the hospital. This unit now performs more than 25,000 dialysis treatments each year.

The personal guidance of Swami Rama has greatly enriched the life of Dr. Prakash and has added meaning and purpose to his life. To repay this debt of gratitude, Prakash has been spreading the teachings of Swami Rama through workshops, seminars, books, videos and audio CDs.

Swami Rama

Swami Rama was born in the Himalayas and was initiated by his master into many yogic practices. His master also sent him to other yogis and adepts of the Himalayas to gain new perspectives and insights into the ancient teachings. At the young age of 24 he was installed as Shankaracharya of Karvirpitham in South India. Swamiji relinquished this position to pursue intense sadhana in the caves of the Himalayas. Having successfully completed this sadhana, he was directed by his master to go to Japan and to the West in order to illustrate the scientific basis of the ancient yogic practices. At the Menninger Foundation in Topeka, Kansas, Swamiji convincingly demonstrated the capacity of the mind to control so-called involuntary physiological processes such as the heart rate, temperature, and brain waves. Swamiji's work in the United States continued for 23 years, and in this period he established the Himalayan International Institute.

Swamiji became well known in the United States as a yogi, teacher, philosopher, poet, humanist, and philanthropist. His models of preventive medicine, holistic health, and stress management have permeated the mainstream of Western medicine. In 1993 Swamiji returned to India where he established the Himalayan Institute

Hospital Trust in the foothills of the Garhwal Himalayas. Swamiji left this physical plane in November, 1996, but the seeds he has sown continue to sprout, bloom, and bear fruit. His teachings, embodied in the words, "Love, Serve, Remember," continue to inspire the many students whose good fortune it was to come in contact with such an accomplished, selfless, and loving master.

Himalayan Institute Hospital Trust

The Himalayan Institute Hospital Trust (HIHT) was conceived, designed, and orchestrated by Dr. Swami Rama, a yogi, scientist, researcher, writer, and humanitarian. The mission of HIHT is to develop integrated and cost-effective approaches to health care and development for the country as a whole, and for under-served populations worldwide.

Swamiji started this project in 1989 with an outpatient clinic of only two rooms. The hospital at HIHT currently has a thousand beds and is serving approximately 10 million people of Garhwal, Kumaon and adjoining areas. The hospital includes a Reference Laboratory, Emergency Wing, Operation Theaters, Blood Bank, Eye Bank, Dialysis Unit, I.C.U., C.C.U., Cath Lab., and a state-of-the-art Radiology Department. The Cancer Research Institute at HIHT is providing radiation therapy in addition to chemotherapy and surgical oncology.

The Rural Development Institute is providing health-care, education, income generation opportunities, water and sanitation programs, adolescent awareness programs and other quality of life improvement programs in the villages of Uttarakhand and adjoining rural areas.

The Himalayan Institute of Medical Sciences has become Swami Rama Himalayan University, a state university promoted by the Himalayan Institute Hospital Trust, and established by the Govt. of Uttarakhand under section 2(f) of UGC Act vide Act no. 12 of 2013. The University runs undergraduate (M.B.B.S.) and postgraduate courses (M.D./

M.S. and Diploma) in 15 disciplines. The medical faculty also conducts paramedical degree courses in Medical Laboratory Technology, Radiology & Imaging Technology, and Physiotherapy. This University includes Himalayan College of Nursing, Himalayan School of Engineering and Technology, and Himalayan School of Management Studies.

The College of Nursing offers a 3-year GNM diploma program, a 4-year B.Sc. program, a 2-year Post Basic B.Sc. program and a 2-year M.Sc. program. The uniqueness of these nursing programs is that nursing students are provided hands-on training both in the community and with the rural population.

Two new departments have been added to the Faculty of Medicine: Dept. of Biosciences and the Dept. of Yoga Sciences and Holistic Health. The Dept. of Biosciences offers undergraduate and postgraduate degree programs in Biochemistry, Microbiology and Biotechnology. The Dept. of Yoga Sciences and Holistic Health currently offers a bachelor's degree program and plans to add a diploma program in the future.

In keeping with Swamiji's mission of integration, the hospital runs outpatient Ayurveda and Homeopathy clinics and the Ayurveda Center provides a residential pancha-karma therapy program for detoxification, rejuvenation and treatment of chronic ailments. The Combined Therapy Program, pioneered by Swami Rama, has been a unique model of holistic health care for more than 30 years. The Combined Therapy Program combines biofeedback, hatha yoga, aerobic exercise, nutrition, breathing, relaxation skills, meditation and other self-awareness techniques.

For information contact:

Himalayan Institute Hospital Trust
Swami Ram Nagar
P.O. Jolly Grant, Dehradun 248016
Uttarakhand, India
91-135-247-1200
pb@hihtindia.org
www.hihtindia.org

Swami Rama Society, Inc.

The Swami Rama Society is a registered, nonprofit, tax-exempt organization committed to Swami Rama's vision of bridging the gap between Western science and Eastern wisdom. The Society was established to provide financial assistance and technical support to institutions and individuals who are ready to implement this vision in the U.S.A. and abroad.

For information contact:
Swami Rama Society, Inc.
5000 W. Vliet St.
Milwaukee, WI 53208 U.S.A.
414-454-0500
info@swamiramasociety.org
www.swamiramasociety.org

OM the Eternal Witness
Secrets of the Mandukya Upanishad
by Swami Rama
ISBN 978-81-88157-43-3, $18.98,
paperback, 202 pages

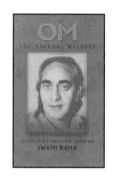

Holistic Living Manual
*The Teachings of Swami Rama of
the Himalayas*
ISBN 978-81-88157-71-6, $18.95,
paperback, 128 pages

Practices of the Himalayan Tradition as Taught by Swami Rama,
volume 1: Breathing & Relaxation
ISBN 978-81-88157-70-9, $9.98,
audio CD

Practices of the Himalayan Tradition as Taught by Swami Rama,
volume 2: yoga nidra
ISBN 978-81-88157-89-1, CDbaby.com
or iTunes.com

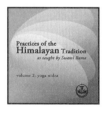

Distributed by Lotus Press, P.O. Box 325, Twin Lakes, WI 53181 U.S.A.,
www.lotuspress.com, 800-824-6396, lotuspress@lotuspress.com

Conscious Living
A Guidebook for Spiritual Transformation
Swami Rama
ISBN 978-188157-03-7, $12.95,
paperback, 160 pages

At the Feet of a Himalayan Master
Remembering Swami Rama, v.1
ISBN 978-81-88157-62-4, $16.98,
paperback, 344 pages

At the Feet of a Himalayan Master
Remembering Swami Rama, v.2
ISBN 978-81-88157-66-2, $18.98,
paperback, 304 pages

At the Feet of a Himalayan Master
Remembering Swami Rama, v.3
ISBN 978-188157-69-3, $18.98,
paperback, 188 pages

Distributed by Lotus Press, P.O. Box 325, Twin Lakes, WI 53181 U.S.A., www.lotuspress.com, 800-824-6396, lotuspress@lotuspress.com

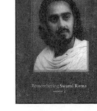

Samadhi the Highest State of Wisdom
Yoga the Sacred Science, vol. one
Swami Rama
ISBN 978-81-88157-01-3, $14.95,
paperback, 256 pages

Sadhana the Path to Enlightenment
Yoga the Sacred Science, vol. two
Swami Rama
ISBN 978-81-88157-68-6, $18.98,
paperback, 310 pages

Sacred Journey
Living Purposefully and Dying Gracefully
Swami Rama
ISBN 978-81-88157-00-6, $12.95,
paperback, 136 pages

Let the Bud of Life Bloom
A Guide to Raising Happy and Healthy Children
Swami Rama
ISBN 978-188157-04-4, $12.95,
paperback, 102 pages

Distributed by Lotus Press, P.O. Box 325, Twin Lakes, WI 53181 U.S.A.,
www.lotuspress.com, 800-824-6396, lotuspress@lotuspress.com